IT HAPPENED TO ME

Series Editor: Arlene Hirschfelder

Books in the It Happened To Me series are designed for inquisitive teens digging for answers about certain illnesses, social issues, or lifestyle interests. Whether you are deep into your teen years or just entering them, these books are gold mines of up-to-date information, riveting teen views, and great visuals to help you figure out stuff. Besides special boxes highlighting singular facts, each book is enhanced with the latest reading list, websites, and an index. Perfect for browsing, there's loads of expert information by acclaimed writers to help parents, guardians, and librarians understand teen illness, tough situations, and lifestyle choices.

1. *Learning Disabilities: The Ultimate Teen Guide,* by Penny Hutchins Paquette and Cheryl Gerson Tuttle, 2003.
2. *Epilepsy: The Ultimate Teen Guide,* by Kathlyn Gay and Sean McGarrahan, 2002.
3. *Stress Relief: The Ultimate Teen Guide,* by Mark Powell, 2002.
4. *Making Sexual Decisions: The Ultimate Teen Guide*, by L. Kris Gowen, Ph.D., 2003.
5. *Asthma: The Ultimate Teen Guide*, by Penny Hutchins Paquette, 2003.
6. *Cultural Diversity: Conflicts and Challenges: The Ultimate Teen Guide*, by Kathlyn Gay, 2003.
7. *Diabetes: The Ultimate Teen Guide,* by Katherine J. Moran, 2004.
8. *When Will I Stop Hurting? Teens, Loss, and Grief: The Ultimate Teen Guide*, by Edward Myers, 2004.
9. *Volunteering: The Ultimate Teen Guide*, by Kathlyn Gay, 2004.
10. *Organ Transplant: A Survival Guide for Recipients and Their Families: The Ultimate Teen Guide*, by Tina P. Schwartz, 2005.
11. *Medications: The Ultimate Teen Guide*, by Cheryl Gerson Tuttle, 2005.

12. *Image and Identity: Becoming the Person You Are*, by L. Kris Gowen, Ph.D., Ed.M., and Molly C. McKenna, Ph.D., 2005.
13. *Apprenticeship*, by Penny Hutchins Paquette, 2005.
14. *Cystic Fibrosis*, by Melanie Ann Apel, 2006.
15. *Religion and Spirituality in America: The Ultimate Teen Guide*, by Kathlyn Gay, 2006.
16. *Gender Identity: The Ultimate Teen Guide*, by Cynthia L. Winfield, 2006.

Religion and Spirituality in America

The Ultimate Teen Guide

Kathlyn Gay

It Happened to Me, No. 15

The Scarecrow Press, Inc.
Lanham, Maryland • Toronto • Oxford
2006

SCARECROW PRESS, INC.

Published in the United States of America
by Scarecrow Press, Inc.
A wholly owned subsidiary of
The Rowman & Littlefield Publishing Group, Inc.
4501 Forbes Boulevard, Suite 200, Lanham, Maryland 20706
www.scarecrowpress.com

PO Box 317
Oxford
OX2 9RU, UK

British Library Cataloguing in Publication Information Available

Library of Congress Cataloging-in-Publication Data

Gay, Kathlyn.
Religion and spirituality in America : the ultimate teen guide / Kathlyn Gay.
p. cm. — (It happened to me ; no. 15)
Includes bibliographical references and index.
ISBN-13: 978-0-8108-5508-3 (hardcover : alk. paper)
ISBN-10: 0-8108-5508-9 (hardcover : alk. paper)
1. United States—Religion. 2. Teenagers—Religious life—United States. I. Title. II. Series.
BL2525.G39 2006
200.973—dc22

2006002837

∞™ The paper used in this publication meets the minimum requirements of
American National Standard for Information Sciences—Permanence of Paper
for Printed Library Materials, ANSI/NISO Z39.48-1992.
Manufactured in the United States of America.

Contents

1	Religious Diversity	1
2	Separation of Church and State	17
3	Mixing Religion with Politics	37
4	Religious Restrictions and Protections	53
5	Religion in Everyday Life	65
6	Religious Rites of Passage	81
7	Lesser-Known Beliefs	95
8	What Agnostics and Atheists Believe	109
9	Getting to Know Others' Beliefs	121
Index		131
About the Author		135

A special thanks to Nissa Beth Gay for conducting interviews and taking photographs in southern California and helping to bridge more than three thousand miles from my office in Florida to the West Coast.—K.G.

1 Religious Diversity

Angel icons. Miracle charms. Incense sticks. Votive candles. Healing poles. Sacred pipes. Food offerings. Halal meat. Kosher food. Turbans. Hijabs. Yarmulkes. Saffron robes. Eagle feathers. Kivas. Longhouses. Temples. Mosques. Churches. Synagogues. Crosses. Crescent-and-star images. Ganesha statues. Religious trinkets. Prayer beads. Nature worship. The Bhagavad Gita. The Bible. The Koran. The Torah. The wind.

I believe there is a higher power at work in my life, but I do not have a name for it.—Amy McKinney[1]

A list of religious and spiritual texts, objects, places of worship, rituals, and ceremonies could fill many pages, and they reflect the wide variety of faiths in the United States. Indeed, the nation has more religious groups than any other country in the world. Increased immigration is expected to contribute even more to religious diversity.

I believe every faith is accurate and that every faith is personal to each individual soul.—Teen post on *Beliefnet.com*[2]

A bindi or dot of red powder on the forehead of this young Hindu girl is a sign of devotion.

If you were to travel throughout the United States, you could find all of the world's major religions and most of the smaller ones represented.[3] In fact, with a little research, you might find a variety of religious groups in your own community, or you might personally investigate another religion.

For example, Timothy Greenberg in Minneapolis, Minnesota, who is Jewish, was curious to learn about his friend's church, so he went with his friend to a Lutheran service. "If they'd been saying things in Hebrew . . . I'd have thought I was in Temple Israel. The atmosphere was the same, a sense of something powerful, uplifting," he told a reporter.[4]

Thousands of teens use the Internet to explore religious and spiritual views. From 1999 through 2005, for example, more than sixteen hundred messages on religion and spirituality were posted on *DiaryProject.com*. Some contributors write about their religions—Buddhism, Christianity, Judaism, other faiths, or spirituality. Belief or nonbelief in God is another topic covered. As one twenty-year-old wrote, "I believe in God, but I don't identify myself with any religion."[5] Others seek advice about their search for a god or something to believe in.

Check it out!

There is no single meaning for the word *religion*. But *ReligiousTolerance.com* offers a broad definition:

> **Religion is any specific system of belief about deity, often involving rituals, a code of ethics, and a philosophy of life. Thus we would consider Christianity, Islam, Judaism, Native American Spirituality, and Neopaganism to be religions. We also include Agnosticism, Atheism, Humanism, Ethical Culture, etc., as religions, because they also contain a "belief about deity"—their belief is that they do not know whether a deity exists, or they have no knowledge of God, or they sincerely believe that God does not exist.[6]**

NATIVE AMERICAN SPIRITUALITY

Some of the oldest spiritual traditions in the world are those of America's indigenous people, sometimes called by such collective names as *Native Americans* or *American Indians* or, as Canadians prefer, *First Nations*. Many Native people keep their beliefs and practices secret in order to protect their heritage and the sacredness of their ceremonies. In fact, some ceremonies cannot be performed if non-Native people are observers—only the initiated are entitled to sacred information.

Others may share some of their beliefs in a general way, but they stress that they do not speak for all Native communities or even closely related ones. For example, Donald Panther-Yates of the Teehahnahmah people, an ancient Native American language group located between the Cumberland Mountains and the Everglades, explained traditional Native spirituality in these general terms:

> Indians don't divide the world into the natural and supernatural. They don't distinguish between the physical and the metaphysical. The visible and the invisible have the same order of being. . . . To an Indian everything is spirit, and all spirit is one. All things are related. "Wind" is just another word for spirit. In my own language, that word is *shah*.

Panther-Yates said that he follows "the old ways in [his] own tribal traditions." Yet, he went on to say, "My great grandfather was Chief Black Fox, a holy man and the last sovereign chief of the Cherokee Nation—I do not pretend to speak for other tribes or other cultures."[7]

Traditional Native spirituality has little resemblance to a formal religion with written dogma and an established place of worship. Here's how one Native practitioner describes the difference between a Native ceremony and a Christian religious observance:

> Rather than going to church, I attend a sweat lodge; rather than accepting bread and toast [*sic*] from the Holy Priest, I smoke a ceremonial pipe to come into Communion with the Great

TOP ORGANIZED RELIGIONS AND NONRELIGIOUS GROUPS

Adherents.com **has collected data to determine the top organized religions, plus the number of nonreligious and atheists in the United States. Estimated total populations in 2004 were as follows: Christianity (224,437,959), nonreligious/secular (38,865,604), Judaism (3,995,372), Islam (1,558,068), Buddhism (1,527,019), agnostic (1,398,592), atheist (1,272,986), Hinduism (1,081,051), Unitarian Universalist (887,703), Wiccan/Pagan/Druid (433,267).[8] Other sources provide different statistics on the number of members in each religious group. For example, Bahá'ís in the United States may total well over 142,000. If you count both adults and children, some 6,000,000 Muslims may live in the United States, according to the Pluralism Project.[9] In short, religious group totals depend on whether all family members are counted, the methods used to conduct surveys, and the year that data are reported.**

> Spirit; and rather than kneeling with my hands placed together in prayer, I let sweetgrass be feathered over my entire being for spiritual cleansing and allow the smoke to carry my prayers into the heavens. I am a Mi'kmaq, and this is how we pray.[10]

There are so many forms of Native American spirituality that it takes an encyclopedia to cover the hundreds of varied traditions. One of the best reference works on the subject is the *Encyclopedia of Native American Religions: An Introduction*, by Arlene Hirschfelder and Paulette Molin. The authors point out that their encyclopedia "tries to accord these Native sacred traditions the respect, status, and rightful place they so richly deserve among other great spiritual traditions."[11]

DIVERSITY AMONG CHRISTIANS

Christians are frequently divided into three main branches: Catholics, Protestants, and Eastern Orthodox. Since colonial

Now You Know!

This symbol of Christianity, called an *ichthys*, was created by early Christians. When meeting another person, a Christian might draw an arc, and if the other person shared the faith, he would complete the symbol by drawing another arc. The ichthys is still used today by many Christians, is often displayed on cars, and is part of jewelry.

The Russian Orthodox, one of the Eastern Orthodox churches, use a cross like this one atop a Russian Orthodox church in Alaska. Photo by the author.

A Latin cross such as this one, on the historic San Buenaventura Mission (still part of a Catholic parish) in Ventura, California, is a symbol of faith for many Christians. Photo by Nissa Gay.

times, Protestants have been the largest branch of Christianity in the United States. However, their numbers have been dwindling in recent years, dropping from 63 percent in 1993 to 52 percent in 2002, according to a study by the University of Chicago's National Opinion Research Center. The study also found that a number of former Protestants now say they have no religion, and among all respondents the nonreligious increased from 9 percent to almost 14 percent.[12]

Although Christianity claims the largest number of believers in the United States, there is no clear definition of who is a Christian or what Christianity means. If you check a few print and online dictionaries, the variety of definitions is evident. *Word Web Online* describes Christianity as "a monotheistic system of beliefs and practices based on the Old Testament and the teachings of Jesus as embodied in the New Testament and emphasizing the role of Jesus as savior."[13]

Webster's New World Dictionary, Third College Edition states that a Christian is "1. a person professing belief in Jesus as the Christ, or in the religion based on the teachings of Jesus.

HALLELUJA OR ALLELUIA?

A "new" Christian group may begin because of an internal conflict, such as a disagreement over a minister or how a building fund is administered. In some cases, a divide can occur over what appears to be a simple matter. In a Colorado church, for example, it was a single word—*halleluja*, or *alleluia* (dictionaries spell it both ways)—that caused a division. The word stems from the Hebrew term for "praise God." The church planned to hang a banner in the sanctuary with the praise word on it. However, one group in the church said it should be spelled beginning with the letter *h*, and the other faction insisted on the *alleluia* spelling. Members on each side insisted that their spelling of the praise word was correct. The debate became so heated that people on both sides complained of harassment. Finally, the church split up over the issue, and the two factions began to meet in separate places, no doubt singing or saying "hallelujah" or "alleluia"![14]

2. a decent, respectable person. 3. having the qualities demonstrated and taught by Jesus Christ, as love, kindness, humility, etc. 4. of or representing Christians or Christianity. 5. humane, decent, etc."

There are at least one thousand different denominations and groups that claim to be Christian, including but not limited to the Amish, Assemblies of God, Baptists, Churches of Christ, Episcopalians/Aglicans, Greek Orthodox, Jehovah's Witnesses, Churches of Jesus Christ Latter Day Saints (Mormons), Lutherans, Mennonites, Methodists, Presbyterians, Roman Catholics, Seventh-Day Adventists, and many others. Some Christian groups assert that they are the only true adherents to the faith. Others accept a variety of groups as Christian.

PRACTICING JUDAISM

Judaism, from which Christianity originally stemmed, has been practiced for centuries, and many American Jews, as historian Jonathan Sarna put it, "think of themselves as kind of one large family."[15] But there have long been divisions or major branches of Judaism in the United States: Orthodox Judaism, Conservative Judaism, Reform/Progressive Judaism, and Reconstructionist Judaism.

Those who practice Orthodox Judaism believe that G-d (a Jewish prohibition forbids spelling out the name of the deity) gave Moses the Torah—the first five books of the Bible.

Leviticus, one of the five books, contains 613 commandments that Jews are bound to observe. Orthodox Jews strictly observe Jewish law and attempt to maintain most of the ancient traditions and practices, although they do not separate themselves from modern society. On the other hand, some Orthodox Jews believe that Jewish laws are absolutes, and they detach themselves from society, much as the Christian Amish do, with distinctive clothing and separate living.

Within the Conservative branch, Jews accept that they should live by Jewish law, which they believe was given by G-d but interpreted by humans. In their view the law can change and adapt to the culture.

Reform Jews believe that though the Torah was inspired by G-d, it was written by various people at different times and then combined. Followers of Reform Judaism believe that Jewish law is open to interpretation and that individuals are free to follow whichever laws, traditions, and customs are appropriate for them. In the words of a Reform rabbi's teenage son, "I find that Judaism is very individualistic, which is good. And I think that if you study Torah and you study the law, you'll find the answers that can help you with your problems. But sometimes that's hard, which is why we have rabbis to help."[16]

A fourth, much smaller movement, Reconstructionist Judaism, also exists and is more liberal than that of Reform Jews. Reconstructionists believe that Judaism is more a social structure than a religious one, and they do not necessarily believe that Jews are chosen people.

Notwithstanding the diverse branches of Judaism, historian Sarna explains that in the United States, "anybody is free, without seeking permission from any chief rabbi or any government office, to open up their own synagogue and to worship God as a Jew in the way that they think best."[17]

An example of worshiping as one thinks best was demonstrated in 2004 when Los Angeles Dodger's baseball star Shawn Greene, who is Jewish, decided to play during Judaism's holiest week, which begins with the Jewish New Year (Rosh Hashanah) and ends with the Day of Atonement (Yom Kippur). Practicing Jews observe Yom Kippur by fasting, refraining from work, and repenting for past wrongdoings. Greene played a game on the evening of Yom Kippur, which began at sundown, and he sat out the game on the next day. "I talked with family and friends and got advice from a lot of people," Greene told a reporter. "When it came down to it, I realized that I just had to do what I feel is right and what's most consistent with my beliefs," Green said. "Everyone has different ways of expressing their beliefs. For me as a Jewish person and a teammate, I feel that this is the right decision for me."[18]

DIVERSITY AMONG MUSLIMS

Non-Muslims in America tend to think of Muslims as one group, all following the same Islamic beliefs in the same way. For example, there is a mistaken perception that Arab Americans are predominantly Muslim. But most Arab Americans are Christians, although in some Arab communities across the United States Muslims predominate while in others there might be a mix of Christians, Muslims, and the nonreligious.

Besides the fact that Arab Americans are not of one religious faith, they do not all share the same culture, originally coming from varied parts of the world. Muslim Arabs may have roots in such countries as Egypt, Iraq, Jordan, Lebanon, Morocco, Palestine, Saudi Arabia, and Syria. In addition, American Muslims could be of African American or West Asian heritage.

Oz, a twenty-year-old American Muslim who was born in Ankra, Turkey, explains that to him practicing the religion is not as important as it is with followers of the faith in other parts of the world. He describes a more secular Islam, in which going to the mosque is a type of social event, going to a place to "meet other people and celebrate" during holidays. Oz notes that in general when someone says that he or she is a Muslim, people "just assume that you're part of this one big group. . . . They don't have an idea about the degrees or differences or variances in Islam."[19]

Islamic variations are underscored in Southern California, where youth whose parents are Muslim immigrants are "changing the face of Islam" in the United States "by combining their faith with the American tradition of diversity," according to a September 2005 report in *Newsweek*. As twenty-five-year-old Haider Javed, a Muslim leader at a youth center put it, "I'm looking at one Pakistani, one white guy, one Palestinian, one African-American guy. . . . They're just standing around, talking. That alone makes me believe America is the perfect place for Islam."[20]

Although there are differences among Muslims, the devout that practice the faith are unified in their sacred obligations, stated in the five pillars of Islam: the *shehada*, a profession of faith that "there is no god but God, and Muhammad is his prophet"; prayer five times each day; *zakat*, giving alms or sharing one's wealth with the poor; fasting daily from sunrise to sunset during the holy month of Ramadan; and the *hajj*, or obligation to go on pilgrimage to Mecca in Saudi Arabia once in one's life, if possible.

WHO CAN LEAD?

While there is no question about the diversity of religions in the United States, that does not necessarily mean that a particular religious group allows diversity within its hierarchy. For example, the Episcopal Church is in an ongoing controversy about the ordination of a gay priest, and a lesbian Methodist minister was defrocked because she publicly disclosed her relationship with another woman.

Some religious organizations have long-standing bans against women in senior authority positions—that is, the top clerical leaders. Within the Roman Catholic, Eastern Orthodox, and Orthodox Judaic groups; numerous Islamic groups; some Protestant denominations, such as the Southern Baptist Convention (SBC); Mormons; and others, women are denied equal rights. Men maintain a patriarchal society and take leadership roles.

In 2000, for example, the SBC issued a resolution stating that a wife should "submit herself graciously to the servant leadership of her husband." Some Southern Baptists who do not believe in this edict pulled away from the denomination. One of those dissenters is former U.S. president Jimmy Carter, who was a longtime member and Sunday school teacher.

After the SBC issued its 2000 resolution, Carter and his wife, Rosalyn, severed ties with the Southern Baptists. Carter pointed out that "this has been a very difficult thing for me. . . . My grandfather, my father and I have always been Southern Baptists, and for 21 years . . . I have maintained that relationship. I feel I can no longer in good conscience do that." He added that he was "familiar with the [biblical] verses [that the SBC] quoted about wives being subjugated to their husbands. . . . In my opinion, this is a distortion of the meaning of Scripture. . . . I personally feel the Bible says all people are equal in the eyes of God. I personally feel that women should play an absolutely equal role in service of Christ in the church."[21]

Gender equity is an issue that has surfaced among some Muslims living in the United States. Traditional Islamic dogma says, among other things, that women should wear modest dress and keep their opinions to themselves. At more than half the mosques in the United States women are not allowed to enter for prayer, or, if they are, they are segregated from the men by a partition or are sent to a separate room or a balcony. But in some instances, women have tried to change this policy.

Consider, for example, Asra Nomani and Asra's mother and teenage niece, who broke a barrier in their mosque in Morgantown, West Virginia. Nomani and her family members plus several other Muslim women entered the main prayer room of their mosque in mid-2004 and prayed in the same space as the men. Although this small group of women continues to pray with the men, others in the congregation do not agree with this practice. Those who support separation of men and women say that it is necessary to prevent sexual distractions and that it helps everyone concentrate on God.

Like numerous other traditional religions, the Eastern Orthodox Church, which includes the Greek Orthodox Church, has a patriarchal structure, and women are denied leadership roles. Women also have secondary roles in various religious celebrations, such as the traditional Epiphany or Theophany (the manifestation of God) ceremony of the Greek Orthodox, each year in January. The ceremony commemorates the baptism of Jesus.

In Orthodox churches around the world, the Epiphany festival usually involves blessing the waters used in church devotions and blessing a local waterway, such as a river, spring, or bayou. In some areas of the United States, a priest plunges a cross in the water and teenage boys or young men dive for it; the one who retrieves the cross is said to be blessed. Usually, girls carry a dove, symbolizing the Holy Spirit, and release it over the waterway. Women by tradition do not participate in the dive, although that is changing in some U.S. cities, such as Long Beach, California, where a girl captured the cross in 2003.

Tradition will no doubt dictate who will be allowed leadership roles in many organized religions for years to come, but some practices may change, as congregations of whatever faith attempt to deal with the influences of U.S. culture, in which equality is an ideal. In addition, unless orthodox religious groups separate themselves from society, they may be affected by the diversity of the current generation of youth, most of whom do not have a strict commitment to a specific doctrine or belief, as several studies show. Reboot, a national network that released a study in 2005 titled *OMG! How Generation Y Is Redefining Faith in the iPod Era* found that participants aged 18–25 were more religiously diverse than the generation before them and were "less likely to identify with traditional Christian denominations." They also were "significantly more likely to see themselves as secular and nondenominational than older Americans."[22] That is evident in the words of a teen known as catolicguy777, who posted his comments on *Beliefnet.com*:

> I was born a practicing but non-believing Catholic, and still go to Mass. However, i believe that every religion is true and good in its own way, and have been leaning towards Unitarian Universalism. In my daily life, i live out the golden rule and i try

> to encourage and respect every person by putting the needs of others before my own. . . . Instead of believing in a personal God, i believe that God is a collective name for all that exists, including energy, or "wind" that keeps the world afloat and transfers from person to person. I believe that good deeds and thoughts create good energy, and bad deeds and bad thoughts create bad energy, so as long as people do selfish or wrong things, this will create bad energy, which will then blow to all of humankind. That's why i think it's so important to live by the golden rule.[23]

NOTES

1. Quoted in John Leland, "Searching for a Holy Spirit," *Newsweek*, May 8, 2000, 62.
2. Spiritpoke, "Whatever Faith You Believe in Will Happen to You," *Beliefnet.com*, August 25, 2005. www.beliefnet.com/boards/message_list.asp?pageID=3&discussionID=409877&messages_per_page=4 (accessed September 10, 2005).
3. Timothy Miller, "Religious Movements in the United States," New Religious Movements, University of Virginia. http://religiousmovements.lib.virginia.edu/essays/miller2003.htm (accessed September 25, 2004).
4. Quoted in John Leland, "Searching for a Holy Spirit," *Newsweek*, May 8, 2000, 62.
5. Karma, "What I Think," *DiaryProject.com*, August 11, 2005. www.diaryproject.com/entries/?86504 (accessed September 14, 2005).
6. "Various Definitions of the Word 'Religion' (None Totally Satisfying)," *ReligiousTolerance.org*. www.religioustolerance.org/rel_defn.htm (accessed October 1, 2004).
7. Donald Panther-Yates, "Remarks on Native American Tribal Religions," March 5, 2001, Georgia Southern University, Statesboro. www.wintercount.org/remark.doc (accessed June 9, 2005); see also, Donald Panther-Yates, "Teehahnahmah (Tihanama) Language," *PanthersLodge.com*. www.pantherslodge.com/tlang.html (accessed February 6, 2006).
8. "Top Ten Organized Religions in the United States," *Adherents.com*. www.adherents.com/rel_USA.html (accessed June 1, 2005).

9. "Pluralism Project—Statistics by Tradition," *Pluralism.org*. www.pluralism.org/resources/statistics/tradition.php (accessed September 9, 2005).

10. Noah Augustine, "Grandfather Was a Knowing Christian," *Toronto Star*, August 9, 2000, quoted on www.religioustolerance.org/nataspir.htm (accessed June 8, 2005).

11. Arlene Hirschfelder and Paulette Molin, *Encyclopedia of Native American Religions: An Introduction* (New York: Facts on File, 2001), vii.

12. Sharon Tubbs, "Protestant Majority Dwindles," *St. Petersburg Times*, August 28, 2004, E1.

13. See www.wordwebonline.com/search.pl?w=christianity (accessed February 14, 2006).

14. Joel Kilpatrick, "Church Splits over Spelling of 'Hallelujah,'" *LarkNews.com*, June 2003. www.larknews.com/june_2003/secondary.php?page=church_split (accessed October 27, 2004).

15. Jonathan Sarna, interview by Rebecca Phillips, "Free-Market Judaism," *Beliefnet.com*, February 2004. www.beliefnet.com/story/142/story_14289_1.html (accessed September 29, 2004).

16. Quoted in Pearl Gaskins, *I Believe In . . . Christian, Jewish, and Muslim Young People Speak about Their Faith* (Chicago: Cricket Books, 2004), 36.

17. Sarna, "Free-Market Judaism."

18. Quoted in Steve Springer and Jason Reid, "Dodger Star Will Observe, and Play on, Yom Kippur," *Los Angeles Times*, September 24, 2004, 1.

19. Quoted in Pearl Gaskins, *I Believe In . . .*, 86–87.

20. Quoted in Lorraine Ali, "A New Welcoming Spirit in the Mosque," *Newsweek*, August 29–September 5, 2005, 52–53.

21. Quoted in Gayle White, "Carter Cuts Ties to 'Rigid' Southern Baptists," *Atlanta Constitution-Journal*, October 20, 2000. www.accessatlanta.com.

22. Anna Greenberg, *OMG! How Generation Y Is Redefining Faith in the iPod Era* (New York: Reboot, 2005), 8.

23. Catolicguy777, "Sharing Faith," June 3, 2005, *Beliefnet.com*. www.beliefnet.com/boards/message_list.asp?pageID=1&discussionID=431856&messages_per_page=4 (accessed September 10, 2005).

2 Separation of Church and State

As I walk through the front doors, several prayerful Christians urge me to join them in worship. . . . I am not in a church, I am walking into my public high school. . . . It is eight o'clock in the morning, I have a headache because I was studying until the early morning . . . and as my classmates implore me to find a new life in Christ all I can think is, "What happened to separation of church and state?"—Michael Hachey[1]

Most Americans who are members of large, mainstream religious denominations seldom worry about being able to worship according to their beliefs. They usually take their religious liberty for granted. But the free expression of religious or spiritual beliefs is a relatively recent concept in human history. As a U.S. State Department publication explains,

> there have been societies that permitted some deviation from state-sanctioned and enforced official religion, but such toleration depended upon the whim of the majority or ruler, and could be withdrawn as easily as it had been given. Religious freedom requires, above all else, the divorce of a nation's religious life from its political institutions, and this separation of church and state, as it is called, is also of relatively recent vintage. One of the great social revolutions that accompanied America's rebellion from England and the adoption of the Constitution and Bill of Rights was the formal separation of church and state, first by the former colonies and then by the federal government.[2]

THE ESTABLISHMENT CLAUSE

The First Amendment to the U.S. Constitution, which is part of the Bill of Rights (the first ten amendments), states that "Congress shall make no law respecting an establishment of religion, or prohibiting the free exercise thereof; or abridging the freedom of speech, or of the press; or the right of the people peacefully to assemble and to petition the Government for redress of grievances." This amendment protects not only religious freedom but also people's right to express themselves and to voice their political and religious beliefs, opinions, and criticisms, without being intimidated by the government.

In the early nineteenth century, Thomas Jefferson, third president of the United States (1801–1809), commented on the establishment clause in the First Amendment when he was asked by the Danbury Baptists Association to proclaim a national day of fasting as a religious observance. Although both previous presidents had made such proclamations, Jefferson refused, explaining in a letter to the Baptists that religion was a matter of individual conscience. He wrote that the First Amendment of the U.S. Constitution was the law of the "whole American people which declared that their legislature should 'make no law respecting an establishment of religion, or prohibiting the free exercise thereof,' thus building a wall of separation between Church and state."[3]

In 1947, Supreme Court Justice Hugo L. Black spelled out his opinion about the establishment clause. Writing the majority ruling in the case of *Everson v. Board of Education*, he noted:

> The "establishment of religion" clause of the First Amendment means at least this: Neither a state nor the Federal Government can set up a church. Neither can pass laws which aid one religion, aid all religions, or prefer one religion over another. Neither can force nor influence a person to go to or remain away from church against his will or force him to profess a belief or disbelief in any religion. No person can be punished for entertaining or professing religious beliefs or disbeliefs, for church attendance or non-attendance. No tax in any amount,

In spite of debates over the "wall of separation," U.S. coins and bills that carry the phrase "In God We Trust" indicate that there is not a distinct separation of church and state.

> large or small, can be levied to support any religious activities or institutions, whatever they may be called, or whatever form they may adopt to teach or practice religion. Neither a state nor the Federal Government can, openly or secretly, participate in the affairs of any religious organization or groups and vice versa. In the words of Jefferson, the clause against establishment of religion by law was intended to erect "a wall of separation between church and State."[4]

Some justices, legal scholars, and others argue that Jefferson did not intend that an absolute wall exist between the affairs of government and religious beliefs and practices. Certainly, the dividing line between church and state has not always been clear, especially when both houses of Congress and state legislatures begin their sessions with prayers offered by chaplains and paid with state funds. Also, the U.S. Supreme Court opens its sessions with "God Save the United States and this honorable Court." In short, conflicts over religion's role in public institutions and the separation of church and state have sparked legal arguments that continue to this day.

Debates over church-state separation also appear in the media, on Internet forums, and in other public places. Lindsey, a twenty-two-year-old in Washington state, posting her views on a student forum, related the issue to how she votes. She explained, "[My] value system revolves around my belief in Jesus—this shapes my morals, and world view, and when you vote you vote based on your view of how things are and should be and on your moral convictions." Therefore, church and state cannot be completely separated, she concluded.[5]

RELIGIOUS SYMBOLS ON PUBLIC PROPERTY

One of the most contentious issues in recent years has been the display of religious symbols on public property—lands and buildings supported by tax funds—and on city stationery and other public documents. Two examples during the 1990s involved Illinois communities: Rolling Meadows and Zion. Both towns had municipal seals that included Christian crosses. In Rolling Meadows, the seal depicted a school, a water tower, a factory, and a church with a cross. The Zion emblem displayed a crown and scepter and a banner reading "God Reigns."

While the Rolling Meadows seal was created as an art project with no religious intent, the Zion seal had been used for nearly one hundred years to reflect the city's original purpose—it was founded as a theocracy, or rule by God through appointed prophets, priests, or similar officials. Courts found both seals contained "sectarian religious imagery [that] has no place on municipal seals."[6] The cities were ordered to remove the religious images on their seals.

A similar case in Redlands, California, was settled in 2004. For nearly forty years, the city's official seal had contained a graphic of a shining cross floating above a church. The seal appeared not only on city stationery but also on "fire fighters' patches, on police badges, on the door of the local library, and elsewhere." After some complaints in 2003 and 2004 by Redlands citizens, an attorney for the American Civil Liberties Union (ACLU) wrote to city officials asking them to remove the symbol because "The law couldn't be any clearer on this. Whether it's an Islamic crescent, a star of David, or a crucifix makes no difference. The government cannot endorse religion. By putting a Latin cross on its official seal, Redlands was effectively telling people of other faiths, and people of no faith, that they were second class citizens."[7] The symbol was removed.

Debates over the Ten Commandments

Numerous debates and court cases have been argued over the placement of plaques or stone carvings containing the Decalogue, or biblical Ten Commandments, in court houses, municipal offices, parks, public schools, and other civic places. Usually, courts determine that these displays violate the constitutional requirement of separating church and state. Of course, not everyone agrees. For example, a teen in Tennessee posted his view on an online forum: "I am a firm supporter of separation of church and state, but it seems that teaching the ten commandments might solve many problems our generation faces. Especially for those whose parents don't care enough to teach them right from wrong. I don't really think its about religion, its more of a morality issue." Another student noted that "morality is not something that can be taught in schools. Not because it's wrong, but because it just wouldn't work. It's something that needs to be taught and reinforced at home, not schools. Parents need to teach their children that, not the taxpayers."[8]

Rachel Cate, a student at Cleveland High School in Bradley County, Tennessee, which had voted in 2002 to allow posting of the Ten Commandments in public places, proposed an alternative. Appearing before a county commission meeting, Cate asked that the Five Pillars of Islam be posted alongside the Decalogue. "This is not only a Christian nation, but a nation for everyone," Cate told the commission. "I think it is discriminatory not to decide on the Five Pillars of Islam . . . just as you decided on the Ten Commandments."[9] The commission did not grant Cate's request.

One highly publicized debate over placement of the Decalogue was the case of Roy Moore, chief justice of the Alabama Supreme Court, who had placed a huge granite monument inscribed with the Ten Commandments in the rotunda of the state judicial building. A federal court ordered that the monument be removed because it endorsed religion, which is unconstitutional. But Moore defied the order, prompting a trial before a court of the judiciary. The nine-member panel unanimously decided that Moore "willfully and publicly" disregarded the order and put himself above the law. In late 2003, the panel removed Moore from office.

Blake Trettien of Frederick, Maryland, had often wondered about a granite carving of the Ten Commandments in his town's public park. He heard about a Decalogue on municipal property in Elkhart, Indiana, that had to be removed because it violated church-state separation. So in spring 2002, while he was a high school senior, he spent a lot of his free time researching the history of the Frederick carving. Then he sent a letter to local officials questioning why a monument inscribed with the Ten Commandments was on city property. Trettien explained, "I outlined the constitutional concerns and requested a response. I didn't really expect one, and went back to my schoolwork. Two weeks later I got a call from an alderman . . . [who] was strongly opposed to doing anything with the monument." Another alderman and the mayor called. Trettien reported, "Apparently my letter had created some sort of a debate within the city that had been going on for weeks. My letter was passed to the legal department, which read it, and agreed with what I had said, that the monument wouldn't stand up to a constitutional test in court." One alderman and the Frederick County Christian Coalition went to the press.

Blake and his family had no idea that a great uproar would follow. Many people in Frederick were livid that anyone would suggest that the Ten Commandments be removed. "They screamed obscenities at me and my parents," Trettien said.

"They called repeatedly at all hours of the day and night. One screamed at my mom, 'How does it feel to raise a Communist?' This was at six o'clock in the morning." One pastor declared Blake was "an evil force" in the county. An editorial in one newspaper called him a "snot-nosed kid," and letters to the editor of some newspapers stated that an eighteen-year-old didn't know what he was doing and that he was engaging in some kind of school project.[10]

As the controversy became more heated, Trettien contacted the ACLU. The organization sent letters to local officials outlining legal precedents for removing the monument. The ACLU also suggested that the land where the monument sits could be sold. When no response came, the organization filed a law suit against the city and county with Trettien and another citizen as plaintiffs. By December 2002, officials in Frederick announced they would sell the land where the Decalogue stands, and the ACLU of Maryland dropped its lawsuit. The 250-by-33-foot parcel of land was sold to the Frederick Eagles, the organization that originally presented it to the city in 1958. (During the 1950s and 1960s, the Fraternal Order of Eagles helped place thousands of Decalogues in villages and towns across the United States, as a promotion for the Charlton Heston movie *The Ten Commandments*.) According to the local newspaper, the Eagles "purchased the property for $6,700 from the city to offer a resolution to a situation they believe they were partially responsible for causing."[11]

Another case focused on an Eagles' donation in 1961 to the state of Texas. This six-foot-high monument, inscribed with the Ten Commandments, and seventeen other structures stand on the grounds of a public twenty-two-acre park that surrounds the Texas capitol. A lawsuit regarding the monument's constitutionality was settled in late June 2005, when the U.S. Supreme Court ruled that the monument was acceptable because it was part of a secular historical display and not intended as an endorsement of a religion.

At the same time as the Texas ruling, the high court issued its decision in a Kentucky case, *McCreary County v. American Civil Liberties Union*. In two Kentucky counties (McCreary and Pulaski), officials had placed framed copies of the Ten Commandments on their court house walls, which prompted a lawsuit by the ACLU. In this case, the Supreme Court ruled that the Decalogues violated the establishment clause because they had been posted strictly for their religious content and then later surrounded by other documents so that they would appear to be part of a historical exhibit. In its majority ruling, the high court said, "An observer would probably suspect the counties of reaching for any way to keep a religious document on the walls."[12]

Because there was no clear-cut ruling about the proper display of the Ten Commandments on public property, many legal experts expect continued litigation. In fact, Christian groups plan to place Decalogues in cities and towns across the United States, and, as the *Washington Post* reported, this will no doubt "spawn more disputes over Ten Commandment displays in parks, town halls and courthouses. . . . The displays are now the front line of a proxy war, standing in for the bigger issue of the place of religion in public life."[13]

Holiday Exhibits

This statement is from a twenty-year-old college student in Santa Cruz, California, who calls herself a Humanist, Pagan, and Spiritualist. Her views about religious symbols in public schools are countered by many Christians who believe and repeatedly say that "Jesus is the reason for the season," so Christmas displays should be religious in nature. Since the Nativity scene commemorates the birth of Christ, many Christians believe that

I went to a public high school, and I hated December. In my creative writing class, our teacher (devout Protestant) had us writing on such blatantly Christian topics I wanted to scream. If schools are going to display symbols of Christmas, they should display ALL symbols of all religious holidays. Not just in December, either.[14]

it should be the primary representation of the Christmas season and the focus of Christmas day.

Holiday exhibits on public property, particularly Christmas displays with a Nativity scene, have prompted many angry debates and court cases. In one case, the U.S. Supreme Court ruled in 1989 that a Nativity display is specifically religious if it stands alone on public property, thus endorsing a religion, which is unconstitutional. The display is allowed on public grounds, however, if it appears with secular decorations such as Santa Claus and his reindeer. There is no question about the legality of religious displays on private property. In some communities, government officials avoid arguments when they require that religious displays appear *only* on private property, such as a home or church lawn.

PUBLIC SCHOOLS AND RELIGIOUS ISSUES

During its earliest days, education in American schools was primarily religious instruction, even after tax-supported schools were established in the mid-seventeenth century. Colleges—both public and private—were also closely linked with religious groups. Only in Virginia were public schools free of church control.

By the early nineteenth century, state legislatures began to pass laws to establish public schools with requirements for public taxation, teacher certification, student attendance, and courses of study. Most state laws prohibited the use of tax funds for religious schools but allowed general religious teaching (such as prayer and Bible reading) in public schools, which meant presenting the beliefs of the majority—Protestants.

As more diverse religious views became represented in the United States in the late nineteenth century and early twentieth century, Catholics, Mormons, Quakers, Jews, and others began to challenge the Protestant dominance. As a result most states passed laws requiring public schools to be neutral on religious matters.

Nevertheless, those laws have frequently been ignored, and some of the most troublesome church-state issues have erupted in public schools, especially since the 1960s. School prayers, Bible readings, Bible clubs, and religious symbols and observances have prompted lawsuits. In addition, controversies focus on whether public funds should be used for voucher systems—using tax money to pay tuition for students to attend private schools, many of which are religious schools.

School Prayer

School prayer may top the list of divisive issues within the past few decades. The high court banned school-sponsored prayers in 1962, even "neutral" prayers that favored no particular religion. Still, prayers in some public schools have continued—that is, until someone protested.

In 1992, the U.S. Supreme Court ruled again on the school prayer issue, in *Lee v. Weisman*. The case centered on a public school practice in Providence, Rhode Island: clergy were asked to say prayers at school graduation ceremonies. The Daniel Weisman family, whose daughter Deborah was graduating from middle school, objected and filed a lawsuit that was eventually heard by the high court, which ruled graduation prayer unconstitutional. Why? Because it promotes religion at a public school event that students are expected to attend even though they may oppose it. As Justice Anthony Kennedy wrote for the majority, "the State may not place the student dissenter in the dilemma of participating or protesting. Since adolescents are often susceptible to peer pressure, especially in matters of social convention, the State may no more use social pressure to enforce orthodoxy than it may use direct means."[15]

In another school prayer ruling, the Supreme Court in 2000 prohibited school officials in the Santa Fe School District in Galveston, Texas, from asking students to use the public address system to lead prayers before football games. Mormon and Roman Catholic families objected and filed a lawsuit (*Doe v. Santa Fe Independent School District*). (The parents' names were not released because of fears of reprisal.) As in the case of *Lee v. Weisman*, "Santa Fe's practice was not a matter of private student speech, but of students speaking on behalf of and at the request of school officials," according to the First Amendment Center. "This factor changed the situation from being one of true private student speech to school-sponsored and -endorsed speech."[16]

Because of these court rulings, many Americans are unaware that student-led prayer groups are allowed on public school campuses under the 1984 Equal Access Act, which was upheld by the high court in 1990. The federal law states that if a public secondary school offers any activities not related to the curriculum, then that school must allow equal access to other group functions without discriminating in regard to religious, political, or philosophical beliefs.

According to the law, a group must be initiated by students, and meetings must be voluntary. There can be "no sponsorship of the meeting by the school, the government, or its agents or employees." No school or government employees can participate in meetings but can monitor them, and the meetings cannot disrupt "the orderly conduct of educational activities within the school." Finally, "nonschool persons" cannot "direct, conduct, control, or regularly attend activities of student groups."[17]

With these criteria in mind, teens in increasing numbers are conducting student-led prayer groups on public high school campuses. For example, in California at Arcadia High School a group of Christian seniors gather outside the school at 6:00 AM, before classes start, to hold prayer meetings. One participant told a reporter that the prayer group had changed her life. "I have a purpose and I see something that is bigger than myself," she said.[18]

Bible Clubs

Bible clubs have also been the subject of school-religion debates, and, like prayer groups, they are allowed under the Equal Access Act and are increasing in number. One such club is the Fraser High School Bible Club, in Detroit, Michigan, where Katie Schneider, president of the club, told a reporter, "I think people thought we were crazy at first—waking up early and coming to school at 6:45 A.M. They knew we were different, and that's what we wanted—to let people know that we are not like everyone else."[19]

When Hans Zeiger was in high school in Pallyup, Washington, he led a Bible club and faced much resistance from school officials. In 2003, at age nineteen, Zeiger's column about the Bible club issue appeared in *RenewAmerica*. He wrote, "I believe in the marketplace of ideas, and if the public schools are to remain alive, they must allow Bible clubs equal footing with the Key Club and the Honor Society. This is what real diversity is all about."[20]

Regardless of support for and legality of Bible clubs, the Equal Access Act has been challenged numerous times, and it has not settled debates over the legislation. In fact, some groups that have long supported the Equal Access Act have protested equal access for controversial student organizations, such as gay/lesbian/bisexual support groups, Wiccans, atheists, Satanists, and others. The Freedom from Religion Foundation, a national group of atheists and agnostics, argues that school Bible clubs are divisive and inappropriate. Annie Laurie Gaylor,

What's Your Opinion?

While school Bible clubs are constitutional, another debate has surfaced over whether the Bible should be taught as literature. Some educators contend that there is a need for an elective Bible course because students do not understand biblical references in English literature, such as those in Shakespeare's plays and other classic works. But there are concerns that a teacher could use the Bible to proselytize, which is unconstitutional. Do you think teachers would try to indoctrinate students if the Bible is taught as literature? What's your opinion?

who leads the group, told *CBS News*, "We get complaints constantly by high schoolers who feel it creates a hostile environment where . . . the children and the students who belong to Bible clubs are being treated as better."[21]

Evolution versus Creationism in Public Schools

Debates over teaching evolution and creationism in U.S. public school science classes have been going on for decades. *Evolution* is the scientific term for facts based on evidence about how plants, animals, and humans have evolved, or changed, over hundreds of thousands of years; it is the basis for the study of biology.

Creationism, as it is debated today, is not based on empirical evidence but on the religious belief that the biblical book of Genesis literally describes how a divine being created the earth and humankind. Two other theories—creation science and intelligent design—take a somewhat different approach. The first presents arguments to disprove evolution, while intelligent design insists that the creation of the world is so complex that divine intervention has to be part of the explanation for the origin of the world.

Many Christians insist that creationism, intelligent design, or creation science should be included in a high school science curriculum. In about two dozen states, legislatures and school boards have attempted to do just that, often encouraged by religious groups who want to end all teaching of evolution. In 2004, for example, Cobb County, Georgia, biology textbooks carried a sticker with this disclaimer: "This textbook contains material on evolution. Evolution is a theory, not a fact, regarding the origin of living things. This material should be approached with an open mind, studied carefully, and critically considered." But a U.S. district judge ordered that the stickers be removed.

In Dover, Pennsylvania, a majority of the school board in the fall of 2004 mandated that the intelligent design theory should be presented as an alternative to evolution. Three school board members quit in protest over the decision, and later in the year, board members who backed intelligent design lost their reelection bids. In addition, the ACLU filed a lawsuit in federal court on behalf of eleven Dover parents, charging that intelligent design promotes a religious belief under the pretext of science. In late December 2005, U.S. district judge John E. Jones III barred the teaching of intelligent design in the school district. Jones declared that there is "overwhelming evidence . . . Intelligent Design is a religious view, a mere re-labeling of creationism and not a scientific theory. . . . It is an extension of the Fundamentalists' view that one must either accept the literal interpretation of Genesis or else believe in the godless system of evolution."[22]

Teens have diverse opinions about this controversy and frequently express their views on teen Internet forums and in chat rooms. In a forum on religion and philosophy, a fifteen-year-old wrote,

> i dont see the big deal? we dont know if evolution is real or not . . . intelligent design just says . . . that a great force made the Earth rather than the big bang theory . . . and that the great force made everything . . . and everyone discusses this at one point or another . . . why cant they pick what they believe? . . . the federal government isnt making this part of the school system . . . they get to [choose] if they want it taught or not.

A high school senior responded with "there's NOTHING WHATSOEVER to back up 'intelligent design,' whilst the creation theory was formed from evidence. i certainly know which theory i believe in."

Another student added, "The theory of evolution hasn't been proved beyond all reasonable doubt, but what scientific theories have?" In his view, evolution is "a hell of a lot more likely than creationism."

One more teen opinion was a bit more ambivalent: "I do agree if we're teaching evolution in schools then maybe [creationism/intelligent design] should be taught too. But if you want to learn that then you should just go to a Catholic school where they do have classes on it."[23]

On another forum, an eighteen-year-old in Hermantown, Minnesota, posted this view: "I personally do not have a

CHECK IT OUT!

One of the most famous court cases regarding evolution was that of a Tennessee teacher, John T. Scopes in 1925. At the time, Scopes taught evolution in his biology class, but a Tennessee law banned any teaching that contradicted "the story of the divine creation of man as taught in the Bible." In a trial court, Scopes was convicted of violating the law. But the Tennessee Supreme Court overturned the conviction. Other court decisions regarding evolution have included

1968—*Epperson v. Arkansas.* The High Court ruled that an Arkansas law that banned the teaching of evolution was unconstitutional because it violated the First and Fourteenth Amendments.

1981—*McClean v. Arkansas Board of Education.* Arkansas passed a law requiring that creation science and evolution receive equal treatment in science classrooms, but a federal judge found the law unconstitutional.

1987—*Edwards v. Aguillard.* Louisiana passed a "Creationism Act" requiring that creationism be taught along with evolution, but the U.S. Supreme Court overturned the law because it endorsed religion and violated the establishment clause.

1990—*Webster v. New Lenox School District.* A teacher claimed that his free speech rights were violated because he was prevented from teaching creationism, but the Seventh Circuit Court of Appeals ruled that school boards can prohibit teaching creation science because it advocates religion.

1994—*Peloza v. Capistrano School District.* A teacher does not have the right to teach creationism in a biology class, the Ninth Circuit Court of Appeals decided.

2001—*LeVake v. Independent School District.* A Minnesota teacher, Rodney LeVake, contended in a lawsuit that his free speech and free exercise of religion rights were violated when he was removed from a classroom because of his criticism of evolution and his creationist views. The lawsuit was dismissed, and the state appeals court upheld the dismissal. LeVake appealed to the Supreme Court, but the high court refused to hear the case.

problem with the Big Bang Theory. I believe that (albeit without certainty) the Big Bang was part of God's creating of the universe. Many say that science disproves the existence of God; I personally believe it re-affirms the existence of God."[24]

School Vouchers

The U.S. Supreme Court has ruled on still another long-standing church-state issue: school vouchers. School voucher programs provide state tax funds to pay tuition for

NOW YOU KNOW!

The biblical account of how the world originated is certainly not the only creation story. Holy texts for a great many religions tell about Earth's beginning. Buddhists, for example, do not believe in a divine creator but say that there are recurring cycles of creation. According to one explanation, "at the beginning of each kalpa (cycle) land forms, in darkness, on the surface of the water. Spiritual beings who populated the universe in the previous kalpa are reborn; one of them takes the form of a man and starts the human race. Unhappiness and misery reigns. This is the interval that we are experiencing today. Eventually, the universe dissolves; all living creatures return to the soul life, and the cycle repeats."[25]

Indigenous people in North America tell numerous sacred narratives about creation, and there are probably as many different accounts as there are tribal groups. Many creation stories begin "in a watery environment from which different beings bring up mud to make the earth," write Arlene Hirschfelder and Paulette Molin, authors of the *Encyclopedia of Native American Religions*. Other stories tell of people who "descend through a hole in the sky to emerge in the present world," or the "world is thought to have resulted from cohabitation between Sky/Man and Earth/Woman."[26]

Multiple books compile creation stories of various religions. You can also find information on the subject by accessing the Internet and using general search terms, such as "creation stories" or "how the world began," or terms relating to a specific religion, such as "Hindu creation stories" or "Celtic creation stories."

elementary and secondary students to attend private or public schools of their choice. Numerous states have set up voucher programs so that students who are enrolled in a low-performing school can transfer to another school. Because voucher programs include payments to many parochial, or religious, schools, critics have charged that this violates the separation of church and state.

In 2002 the high court ruled in a Cleveland, Ohio, case (*Zelman v. Simmons-Harris*) that the Cleveland voucher program did not violate the establishment clause of the First Amendment. The high court determined that a voucher program is constitutional if it provides "true private choice" with both secular and religious school options. Parents who receive government funds must make an independent choice regarding where to send their children to school—public or private.

Yet law and education experts say that the *Zelman* decision will probably not be the final word on school vouchers, because the issue has to be determined in the states. Many state constitutions forbid using tax funds to help support religious institutions, as is the case in Florida. The Florida constitution clearly says that "no revenue . . . shall be taken from the public treasury directly or indirectly in aid of any church, sect or religious denomination or in aid of any sectarian institution." A state appeals court ruled in August 2004 that Florida's voucher program, which began in 1999, violates the Florida constitution because it uses tax money to send students to religious schools. The state appealed the decision to the state supreme court, which in early 2006 ordered the state to shut down its voucher program. The court ruled that the state constitution requires a free and uniform public school system, and it further stated that the legislature had no authority to set up a voucher program.

NOTES

1. Michael Hachey, "Separation of Church and State? Not Where I Live," *AlterNet.org*, October 2, 2002. www.alternet.org/wiretap/14214/ (accessed May 31, 2005).
2. U.S. Department of State, *Rights of the People: Individual Freedom and the Bill of Rights*, chap. 2. http://usinfo.state.gov/products/pubs/rightsof/modern.htm (accessed May 24, 2005).
3. Quoted in H. Frank Way, *Liberty in the Balance: Current Issues in Civil Liberties* (New York: McGraw-Hill, 1981), 71.
4. "Jefferson's Wall of Separation Letter," *USConstitution.net*. www.usconstitution.net/jeffwall.html (accessed September 27, 2004).
5. Lindsey, "America Is Not a Christian Country," Student Center Forums, September 8, 2005. http://teenforums.studentcenter.org/viewtopic.php?t=175026&postdays=0&postorder=asc&start=15# (accessed September 9, 2005).
6. Quoted in William Grady, "City Seals Ruled Unconstitutional," *Chicago Tribune*, March 20, 1991, 1.
7. Quoted in "Separation of Church and State: The Use of Religious Symbols by Municipalities and States," *ReligiousTolerance.org*, www.religioustolerance.org/sep_c_s1.htm (accessed October 2, 2004).

8. Tom_in_TN, "Ten Commandments," May 21, 2001, *Beliefnet.com*. http://images.beliefnet.com/boards/message_list.asp?boardID=487&discussionID=50801 (accessed September 11, 2005).

9. Quoted in Associated Press, "Teen Asks Tennessee County to Display Islamic Pillars," April 2, 2002, *FreedomForum.org*. www.freedomforum.org/templates/document.asp?documentID=15990 (accessed September 11, 2005).

10. Blake Trettien, "Thou Shalt Defend Thy First Amendment," *Free Thought Today*, January/February 2003. www.ffrf.org/fttoday/janfeb03/index.php?ft=trettien.html (accessed September 30, 2004).

11. Chris Patterson, "Monument Sale Ends Controversy," December 31, 2002. www.gazette.net.

12. Quoted in David Stout, "Commandment Displays Allowed on Some Government Property," *New York Times*, June 28, 2005, 1.

13. Alan Cooperman, "Christian Groups Plan More Monuments," *Washington Post*, June 28, 2005, A6.

14. StarEagle2002, "What Do You Believe about Holiday Decorations in Public Schools?" *Beliefnet.com*. December 7, 2004, www.beliefnet.com/story/57/story_5778_1.html (accessed September 10, 2005).

15. Anthony J. Kennedy, *Lee et al. v. Weisman*, argued November 6, 1991, decided June 24, 1992. http://supct.law.cornell.edu/supct/html/90-1014.ZS.html (accessed October 10, 2004).

16. First Amendment Center, "Religious Liberty in Public Schools—School Prayer." www.firstamendmentcenter.org/rel_liberty/publicschools/topic.aspx?topic=school_prayer (accessed October 10, 2004).

17. The text of the Equal Access Act is available at http://assembler.law.cornell.edu/uscode/html/uscode20/usc_sup_01_20_10_52_20_VIII.html (access February 6, 2006).

18. Quoted in K. Connie Kang, "No Separation of Students from Prayer on Campus," *Los Angeles Times*, September 5, 2005. www.latimes.com.

19. Quoted in Marisa Schultz, "Metro Schools' Bible Clubs Thriving with Spirited Teens," *Detroit News*, February 8, 2004. www.detnews.com.

20. Hans Zeigler, "The Battle for Public School Bible Clubs," *RenewAmerica.us*, May 10, 2003. www.renewamerica.us/columns/zeiger/030510 (accessed September 10, 2005).

21. "When Bible Study Is Controversial," *CBSNews.com*, July 31, 2004. www.cbsnews.com/stories/2004/07/31/eveningnews/main633260.shtml (accessed September 10, 2005).

22. Quoted in Michael Powell, "Judge Rules against 'Intelligent Design,'" *Washington Post*, December 21, 2005, A1.

23. Posted on Futazi Message Board and Chats, Religion and Philosophy, August 13, 2005. www.futazi.com/futaziforum/showthread.php?t=219&goto=nextoldes (accessed September 11, 2005).

24. Posted on GovTeen Forums, Big Bang Theory Proven—Religion Takes Back Seat, February 12, 2003. http://forums.govteen.com/showthread.php?t=16149 (accessed September 12, 2005).

25. B. A. Robinson, "Beliefs of Various Faith Groups about Evolution and Creation," *ReligiousTolerance.org*, July 31, 2002. www.religioustolerance.org/ev_denom.htm (accessed November 1, 2004).

26. Arlene Hirschfelder and Paulette Molin, "Creation Accounts," *Encyclopedia of Native American Religions* (New York: Facts on File / Checkmark Books, 2001), 59.

3 Mixing Religion with Politics

> **The president speaks like he is some sort of prophet put on earth to do God's work, no matter how many people's rights he has to ignore on the way. . . . He is in power to protect our rights, not destroy them.—Posting on a teen forum[1]**

In spite of Supreme Court decisions regarding separation of church and state and rulings about religious practices in public places, religious views about social issues have frequently been mixed with politics in the United States. In the past, for example, religious groups argued in the public arena for and against slavery. And clergy made their political views known—pro or con—regarding a woman's right to vote. Amendments to the U.S. Constitution established laws

> **Religion (at least some religions) and politics are totally inseparable, and both fail when they are separated. Christianity is an intrinsically political faith, and there is no Christianity without politics. —Nate, 20, Huntington, Indiana[2]**

regarding both of these issues. The Thirteenth Amendment abolished slavery, and the Fourteenth and Fifteenth Amendments protected the citizenship and voting rights of blacks. The Nineteenth Amendment gave women voting rights.

In more recent history, segregation and civil rights were heated political issues with religious leaders weighing in with their opinions. There is no more prominent example than the Reverend Martin Luther King Jr. and his stance from the pulpit and in his speeches; along with using arguments based on the Constitution and the promise of equality, he used biblical pronouncements to make his case for civil rights for people of color. During his time (the 1950s and 1960s) many Christian denominations, like much of U.S. society, were segregated by race, and some congregations believed that racial integration was a sin. Indeed, the SBC encouraged its white congregations to boycott restaurants and hotels that served people of color, although the church group eventually changed that policy and apologized for its racist attitudes.

Today, morality-based politics often split people into two general camps, broadly labeled *conservative* and *liberal*. Those two camps include people with varied religious backgrounds, but since Christianity is the dominant religion, Christians usually have the strongest voice. Conservative Christians often press for a moral code based on a literal interpretation of the Bible, with evangelicals stressing that people be "born-again"—that is, accept Jesus Christ as their savior. Liberal religious groups, on the other hand, are likely to stress social concerns. They usually respect diverse religious beliefs, recognizing common threads among varied theological views.

These differing views often trigger heated political debates today, particularly when it comes to private and personal behavior. Some preachers, religious leaders, politicians, and voters argue, for instance, that homosexual relationships, abortion, stem cell research, and the right to die should be legally banned. Others contend that private matters should be determined by individuals and that the nation's moral problems are much more broad-based and should center on such issues as war, public health, poverty, and economic justice.

What's Your Opinion?

In the political arena, numerous conservative Christians demand that the nation's people live by Christian values, and they believe that these values should dominate governmental actions. Some would like to establish a theocracy—a rule by God through self-appointed prophets or officials who claim to have direct communication with God. Yet many Americans live by moral or ethical values that may not be tied to a Christian doctrine or any other religious doctrine. In the view of many citizens, public policies should reflect the diversity of religious and nonreligious views and recognize that morality is not always shaped by religion. What's your opinion?

HOMOSEXUALITY

Only in recent times has homosexuality been discussed openly; it has become a religious-political issue in families, schools, religious institutions, workplaces, and government. The topic is a common one on Internet teen forums, and posts go on for page after page with unequivocal opinions, such as this eighteen-year-old's comments on GovTeen forums:

> The truth of the matter is that God creates perfectly but the devil perverts God's intentions and design. . . . One of his tactics is to introduce people to homosexuality. The shame and guilt that accompany this lifestyle make those who live it easy prey for the enemy of God to control and destroy.
>
> For that reason, we must shed light on the deception that homosexuality is an acceptable choice that doesn't carry with it any consequences. We must not allow any more people to be deceived, and we must work to help free those who are caught up in this lifestyle.[3]

The opposite position is taken by some who post on this forum, as was the case with a twenty-one-year-old who believes that quoting biblical passages to argue against homosexuality cannot be proven "false anymore than they can be proven true. The concepts are based on faith: some have it and some don't. The bible is no justification for discrimination and harassment. That's all. My point is not to bash the bible or people's faith, but to point out it is just that: faith. It is true to themselves but questionable to others."[4]

In many instances gay or lesbian youth begin to question their religious convictions when they are rejected by their families and church members who view homosexuality as a sin. Other religious youth who have homosexual friends have been faced with a choice: stay in a church that denounces homosexuality or remain loyal to their friends.

At Montgomery Blair High School, in Silver Spring, Maryland, an award-winning online school newspaper reported in 2005 that gay and lesbian youth are confused and frustrated when religious organizations pronounce them "sinful" and exclude them from services or make them feel uncomfortable within their congregations. Because of the teachings of her Baptist church, a lesbian teen declared, "It doesn't feel right anymore. I just feel awkward there." A gay Catholic teen explained, "I'm following a religion that teaches that, no matter what, I'm going to end up in hell because I'm not straight." That has prompted him to question his faith. Another gay teen has decided that he will not be a part of any organized religion and will just be himself. Nevertheless, these teens say they still believe in God.[5]

At some colleges and high schools students have conducted a Day of Silence or a T-shirt campaign to advocate tolerance and acceptance of homosexual students, attempting to prevent bullying and brutal physical attacks on gays and lesbians. At Homewood-Flossmoor, a suburban Chicago high school, a T-shirt campaign in the spring of 2005 carried the slogan "Gay? Fine by Me," an annual effort that began at Duke University in 2003. But the campaign morphed into a T-shirt "war" of sorts. Some of the Christian students at the school began wearing

T-shirts circulated by a local church; the shirts carried the message "Crimes against God" on the front, and on the back, words highlighted "discrimination against . . . my ten commandments, my prayers, my values, my faith and my God." The Christian group said they had the right to voice their opinions just as others did.[6]

In spite of the opposing views, the competing T-shirts did not cause a lot of friction. School officials declared all the messages were a matter of free speech and would be allowed as long as the two sides did not create a disruption or interfere with education.

In efforts to prevent abuse and discrimination against people considered "different" from the mainstream, the Southern Poverty Law Center (SPLC), headquartered in Montgomery, Alabama, created a declaration of tolerance. A person who signs a SPLC declaration pledges in part "to have respect for people whose abilities, beliefs, culture, race, sexual identity or other characteristics are different from my own." The pledge is being used by the We Are Family Foundation, which began as a response to the tragedy of September 11, 2001. As part of its efforts to support victims of intolerance, the foundation produced and distributed an elementary school video featuring one hundred popular cartoon characters, such as SpongeBob SquarePants, Winnie the Pooh, Big Bird, Barney, and others, who sing songs with tolerance-based themes.

James Dobson, leader of a national Christian group called Focus on the Family, pointedly criticized the video while speaking to conservative Christian groups in Washington, D.C., in early 2005. Dobson later reported that "while the video is harmless on its own, I believe the agenda behind it is sinister." He believes that the "childhood symbols are apparently being hijacked to promote an agenda that involves teaching homosexual propaganda to children."[7] Dobson has also criticized the SPLC's tolerance pledge, asserting that it promotes homosexuality and that the concepts of diversity and tolerance "are almost always buzzwords for homosexual advocacy," as he put it in his newsletter.[8]

Jennifer Holladay, director of SPLC's tolerance education programs, stated that "God's love has room for everyone. How unfortunate that Dr. Dobson and many of his followers can't muster simple tolerance for their gay and lesbian brothers and sisters. I believe in Dr. Dobson's right to hold and express his beliefs. I also believe that our democracy allows for both Dr. Dobson and a child with two moms."[9]

SAME-SEX MARRIAGE

An even more contentious religious-political issue is same-sex marriage. Like the general topic of homosexuality, teens often weigh in with their views. Here are just a few comments from a UNICEF website that asked the question "Gay marriages—is it right?":

> I am against gay marriage because it takes away the traditional meaning of the word "marriage." Gay marriage is, essentially, an oxymoron. Give gays civil unions, domestic partnerships, or whatever other title they want—but to call their relationship a "marriage" is simply improper English.
>
> —A nineteen-year-old girl in the United States

> I don't mind gay people, and I don't discriminate against them, but I am against marriage. Two people like that are practically against the human nature.
>
> —A fifteen-year-old girl in the United States

> Our world has adapted to our ever changing society before, can we not adapt again to provide other couples, that happen to be same sex with the same rights straight couples have? A past Prime Minister of Canada once said that the state has no business in the bedrooms of its people.
>
> —A fifteen-year-old girl in Canada

> I know in the traditional way, the word *marriage* applies to a man and a woman. But the world is evolving all the time,

> people change, mentalities change. In the traditional sense, there was also no divorce. And yet this has changed with time. So why not allow gays to get married too? I don't think it would be a wrong thing to do. But what I also think is that a lot of countries are not ready for this yet, as the majority of the population isn't exactly "gay friendly."
>
> —An eighteen-year-old girl in Brazil[10]

Another website asked a similar question: "Is same-sex marriage wrong?" Responses also reflected both sides of the debate, with some posts simply saying, "Yes, it's wrong," to another declaring, "Marriage shouldn't be decided by the government PERIOD, no matter what the couple is."[11]

In an online issue of *Teen Voices,* Christine Storgeoff, seventeen, of Canada wrote, "In my opinion, society's view on sexual orientation—that being gay, lesbian, or bisexual is abnormal and that homosexuals should be persecuted—is warped and bigoted. It reminds me of the witch-hunts back in medieval times when people were publicly humiliated for being different. The fact that hundreds of years have passed since people were burned at the stake for being different should suggest that it is time for discrimination to stop."[12]

Thousands of clergy and laypeople have spoken out against same-sex marriage. Many religious groups contend that homosexuality is not a genetic trait; thus, on that basis, gay men and lesbians do not qualify for the legal protections and civil rights granted minority groups. Indeed, President George W. Bush called for an amendment to the U.S. Constitution that, in effect, discriminates against people who happen to be homosexual, by making gay marriage illegal. According to numerous polls, a majority of Americans favors such an amendment, which would define marriage as being that between a man and a woman.

As of spring 2005, eighteen states had passed state constitutional amendments that ban gay marriage; some also deny civil rights to homosexual couples. Religious organizations are urging other states to follow suit, claiming that God ordained that marriage be between a man and a woman.

To some supporters of same-sex marriage or homosexual civil unions, what is or is not God-ordained is arguable, since diverse religions and secular groups have different claims for who or what a supreme being is and what that being has decreed. As a twenty-five-year-old counselor in Oregon put it, "How absolutely arrogant it is for some people to tell others whom they should love and choose to spend their life with."

What about the impacts on youth who have been raised in households in which their parents are gay men or lesbians? Homosexual couples can legally have children through adoption, use of donor sperm, or in vitro fertilization. But they are not legally allowed to marry. How do teens react to such a contradiction? An article posted on the website *Kids and Politics: A Project by Connect for Kids* presented the views of several teens.

Cleopatra Bezis, who is the adopted daughter of two lesbian moms, believes homosexual or transgender people should "have the option. . . . Why should we breed discrimination when we should be fighting against it?" Bezis explained that her mothers "currently are not planning to get married, but they also do believe that they should have the option or the right."

A college student, Quinn Duffy, who has two dads (one he calls his "stepfather"), declared that all teens, no matter what their family structure, "should be concerned with gay marriage. . . . If they stand for 'liberty and justice for all,' they must support gay marriage. . . . The political situation now appears that the choice will be between legalizing gay marriage or banning it in a constitutional amendment, and I don't think anyone wants to be known as the generation that codified hate into the constitution."[13]

ABORTION ISSUES

As is well known, many Americans have strong beliefs—pro and con—about abortion. Both views may be based on religious or moral values, and these ideas have become part of the public discourse. For example, some teens may declare that abortion is absolutely wrong or evil. Conversely, other teens contend that women should be able to choose whether or not to have an abortion.

Frequently, abortion arguments stem from conflicting concepts about "personhood"—that is, when a fetus becomes a person. Roman Catholics and evangelical Protestants are just two groups that contend that a human is developing from conception on and should be protected. However, according to Ronald M. Green, chair of the Department of Religion at Dartmouth College,

> [that] is not the view of Judaism or Islam, which, even in their most conservative expressions, tend to hold a developmental or "gradualist" view of moral personhood. It is not the view of most Buddhists and Hindus. Despite their moral discomfort with abortion, these traditions have a much more nuanced set of views about when human life becomes protectable. It is not even the view of Mormons, many of whom hold that embryos do not become protectable until implantation occurs. Most importantly, it is not the view of the hundreds of millions of people in this country and around the world who are not instructed by specific Christian religious teachings.[14]

The mix of political-religious views on abortion are not new. In early America, a pregnant woman usually could choose to have an abortion before quickening, or the time when the fetus first moves in the womb. But by the mid-1800s, an increasing number of middle-class married women—primarily white Protestants—were aborting pregnancies to limit the size of their families. As white birth rates declined, some Protestant leaders feared they would be outnumbered by immigrant groups of other religions (particularly Roman Catholics) and by people of color. "Antiabortion activists pointed out that immigrant families, many of them Catholic, were larger and would soon outpopulate native-born [whites] and threaten their political power," writes Leslie J. Reagan in her book *When Abortion Was a Crime*.[15] Because of this view, native-born whites began to call for abortion bans.

Other groups wanted to prohibit abortion because of health hazards. In addition, many of these groups were worried about the campaign for women's rights at that time, and antiabortionists thought that women should stay in traditional roles as wives and mothers. Thus, by 1900 most states outlawed abortions except to save a pregnant woman's life.

It was not until the 1960s that women's rights organizations began efforts to change restrictive state abortion laws. Abortion was legalized nationally in 1973 with the U.S. Supreme Court decision in *Roe v. Wade*. That ruling struck down state laws that severely restricted abortion, declaring such laws unconstitutional because they did not protect a woman's right of privacy. Although the right of privacy is not explicitly mentioned in the Constitution, "a right of personal privacy, or a guarantee of certain areas or zones of privacy, does exist under the Constitution," the Court ruled.

Ever since the *Roe v. Wade* decision, the pro and con public debate over abortion has continued unabated, often with religious groups choosing one side or the other in political campaigns. Candidates for elected office are often asked whether they are for or against abortion, and voters sometimes make their decisions based on this one issue.

STEM CELL RESEARCH ISSUES

Along with focusing on the abortion debate, religious groups and individuals who believe personhood begins at conception have taken strong stands against embryonic stem cell research and have inserted their religious views into political decision making. For example, the National Conference of Catholic Bishops, the American Life League, the National Right to Life Committee, and other groups that call themselves pro-life have lobbied members of Congress to pass legislation restricting research on stem cells. Why? Because in the laboratory, stem cells are extracted from fertilized eggs that are only a few days old, which destroys the embryo—a sin akin to murder according to religious groups that oppose this research.

Yet many of the embryos used in research were developed through in vitro fertilization. That is, women unable to conceive have gone to fertility clinics where a woman's egg is extracted and fertilized with a partner's sperm in a petri dish, then placed into the woman's womb to develop. Usually, in such a process, numerous embryos are created, and those not implanted are frozen. With the consent of donors, unused embryos may be discarded or sent to laboratories for stem cell research. Because stem cells have the potential to develop into many different cell types in the body, researchers hope to find ways to cure such serious illnesses as diabetes, Parkinson's disease, heart damage, and other ills.

However, because of organized opposition to stem cell research, President Bush, on August 9, 2001, banned the use of federal money to study stem cells, except for those derived from frozen embryos that had already been taken from fertility clinics. This means that researchers working on stem cells created after August 9, 2001, may not use any federal grant money to pay for expenses. To support this position and call on the federal government to ban all research using human embryos, teens took part in the annual March for Life in Washington, D.C., in January 2002. "I got involved because I hated the stereotype that young people have no passions or convictions," Dan Stephens from Los Angeles told a reporter. "My passion in coming out here is for justice. Our society can't stand for injustice, even to persons still in the womb." Katy Binskin of Dayton, Ohio, declared, "We have to stand up for what is right."[16]

Another view comes from eighteen-year-old Allison Blass, who is a diabetic and advocate for the Juvenile Diabetes Research Foundation. She believes that

> the promise of a cure by stem cells is very exciting, but as a pro-lifer, I have had to wrestle with this issue. At the end of the day, I do not believe that the embryo is being wasted, such as it is in an abortion. This embryo has the potential to help alleviate the suffering of hundreds of people. There are about 400,000 frozen embryos in in vitro fertilization clinics, and most will be discarded in the trash. Why not honor the potential of an embryo by helping others, especially if the embryo has no chance of having a life of its own? Why not use it to give back a life?[17]

Without federal support, funds may not be sufficient or available at most universities and other institutions to maintain expensive stem cell research. But that may change. In 2004 and 2005, bills were introduced in Congress to ease the federal ban somewhat, and some prominent congressional conservatives, such as Senator Orin Hatch of Utah and Senator Arlen Specter of Pennsylvania, have declared their support for expanded stem cell research funded by the federal government. In 2005, polls by *ABCNews.com* and *Beliefnet.com* show that the majority of Americans supports increased research and government funding for stem cell research.[18]

Acting independently of the federal government, some states already have passed legislation to finance stem cell and related research. Californians, for example, passed a bond measure in 2005 that provides $3 billion for human embryonic stem cell experiments.

RIGHT-TO-DIE ISSUES

Only a few decades ago, terminally ill people had few choices to make about their care. There were no extraordinary means available to extend life. But today scientific advances and medical technology have helped people live longer, and they have also prolonged dying. As a result religion, politics, and the courts have become entwined in debates about whether people have the right to die or whether they should be kept alive artificially with such equipment as feeding tubes, hydration, and ventilators. These debates are especially heated and complex when people have to make a decision regarding a family member who is near death or in a persistent vegetative state, a condition in which reflex actions occur but the cerebral cortex, or thinking and memory part of the brain, does not function.

During the 1970s and 1980s two highly publicized and tragic persistent vegetative state cases, those of Karen Ann Quinlan and Nancy Cuzan, prompted much debate about the right to die. Both young women were kept alive by artificial means for years but were finally allowed to have their life support systems legally removed. However, no case within the past two decades has created as much widespread political and religious controversy as that of Floridian Terri Schiavo.

Schiavo had a heart attack at age twenty-seven. Her brain was deprived of oxygen, which led to brain damage and a permanent coma—a persistent vegetative state. She existed in this condition for fifteen years, and for much of that time her husband, Michael, tried a variety of therapies, believing that she might improve. However, after numerous tests and consultations with doctors, Michael was convinced that there was no cure for Terri, and he asked that a tube be removed that delivered nutritional liquid and hydration to his wife's body. Michael declared that Terri would not wish to live in that condition. Although Terri herself had made no written statement—that is, no living will or advance directive—about her end-of-life decisions, state courts ruled several times over the years that Terri's wishes as articulated by her husband and close friends should be honored.

All across the United States and around the world, people expressed their opinions about Terri's condition and what should or should not be done. On *Diaryproject.com*, a fifteen-year-old asked those on the teen forum what they thought about the Schiavo case and "how it impacts religious and political views of our time? is it against god and country or the right thing 2 do?" Responses varied:

> I am really impartial. . . . I definitely don't like the idea of anyone starving to death. . . . I do wish that they would have had more time. Why not just put the feeding tube back in for a week or so, allow her to regain her strength then do some tests?

> there is a difference between being alive, and actually living. who wants a passive existence? even if she is only considered severely handicapped, it interferes with any type of life she could have. im going to make certain that everyone knows i want them to kill me if i ever am in that condition

> is a quality of life still left in her even if it is diminished greatly. . . . Who are we to rob her of that because "we wouldn't want to live that way"?

> This is one of those decisions that's just not for the public to make. . . . These kind of cases are very private, very painful, and very controversial.[19]

Terri's tube was removed on March 18, 2005. But her parents and brother and sister, who disagreed with Michael Schiavo, wanted the tube reinserted, which resulted in more court battles and the involvement of the U.S. Congress, President George W. Bush, Florida governor Jeb Bush, and countless religious groups presenting their views in front of television cameras. Most of the people involved, including members of Congress, the president, and governor, had never seen Terri Schiavo and had no expert knowledge of her medical condition. Even Senator Bill Frist, a former heart surgeon who had never examined Schiavo, claimed that video clips of Schiavo convinced him that she was not in a vegetative state. Doctors who had examined Schiavo and her brain scans continued to maintain that her condition was hopeless, but they were seldom heard during the media circus surrounding the case. On March 31, 2005, less than two weeks after her tube was removed, Terri Schiavo's body died.

Many who thought that Schiavo's feeding tube should be reinserted accused her husband, doctors, courts, and judges of allowing Terri to die of starvation and dehydration. But medical experts argued that a feeding tube is a medical device that mechanically pumps nutrients and hydration into the body—no different from a ventilator that artificially provides air to the lungs.

The mix of religion and politics in the debate over Schiavo included death threats and hate mail sent to Michael Schiavo and Judge George Greer, who presided over the case. Yet, a majority of Americans believe that end-of-life decisions should be private family matters free of government intrusion. According to a *CBS News* poll taken immediately after Terri Schiavo's death, 82 percent of Americans said that government should not have intervened in the case. At the same time, pro-life activists, who are also involved in abortion and stem cell issues, believe that government has an obligation to protect life and intervene when there is no written directive regarding a person's end-of-life wishes. These two sides continued their debate even after an autopsy showed that Schiavo's brain had atrophied, that she was blind, and that there was no way she could have recovered. The differences are not likely to be settled soon.

NOTES

1. Posted on Scarleteen Boards, Religion in Politics, October 10, 2004. www.scarleteen.com/forum/Forum8/HTML/000833.html (accessed November 7, 2004).
2. Posted on Teen Forums, Politics and Religion, October 20, 2004. http://teenforums.studentcenter.org/viewtopic.php?t=86737# (accessed November 2005).
3. Posted on GovTeen Forums, May 9, 2005. http://forums.govteen.com/showthread.php?t=120614 (accessed September 12, 2005).
4. Posted on GovTeen Forums, September 9, 2005. http://forums.govteen.com/showthread.php?t=120614&page=21&pp=15 (accessed September 12, 2005).
5. Quoted in Pria Anand, ed., "Staying True to Ideology and Identity," *Silver Chips Online*, April 13, 2005. http://silverchips.mbhs.edu/inside.php?sid=5308 (accessed May 3, 2005).
6. Kati Phillips, "Fine by All?" *Daily Southtown*, April 19, 2005. www.dailysouthtown.com; also see Jennifer Skalka, "High School Teens Face a Gay T-shirt Showdown," *Chicago Tribune*, April 19, 2005.
7. Skalka, "High School Teens."
8. James Dobson, "Setting the Record Straight," *Dr. Dobson's Newsletter*, February 2005. www.family.org/docstudy/newsletters/a0035339.cfm (accessed April 22, 2005).
9. "Religious Right Attacks Tolerance Pledge," *SPLC Report*, March 2005, 7.
10. Posted on Voices of Youth, Gay Marriages—Is It Right? March 13–14, 2005. www.unicef.org/voy/discussions/showthread.php?t=1770 (accessed September 12, 2005).
11. Posted on Teen Message Boards, September 1–16, 2005. www.teenspot.com/boards/showthread.html?t=224001&page=1&pp=20 (accessed February 6, 2006).

12. Christine Storgeoff, "Ban Bigotry, Not Same-Sex Marriage," *Teen Voices Online*, September 2005. www.teenvoices.com/issue_current/tvspecial_bigotry.html (accessed September 13, 2005).

13. Quoted in Robert Capriccioso, "Teens Speak Out on Gay Marriage," *Kids and Politics: A Project by Connect for Kids*, April 5, 2004. www.kidsandpolitics.org/Articles/teens_speak_out_on_gay_marriage.htm (accessed April 23, 2005).

14. Ron Green, "Stem Cell Smackdown: Part Three," *Beliefnet.com*. www.beliefnet.com/story/153/story_15349_1.html?rnd=49#rongreen_040929 (accessed April 23, 2005).

15. Leslie J. Reagan, *When Abortion Was a Crime: Women, Medicine, and the Law in the United States, 1867–1973* (Berkeley: University of California Press, 1997), 11.

16. Quoted in Jason Pierce, "Teen Prolifers Protest Embryonic Stem Cell Research," *CBSNews.com*, January 21, 2002. www.cnsnews.com/ViewCulture.asp?Page=%5CCulture%5Carchive%5C200201%5CCUL20020121e.html (accessed September 11, 2005).

17. Quoted in "JDRF Teen Volunteer Joins Panel on Ethics of Stem Cell Research," *Teen Talk at DiabetesStation.com*, May 12, 2004. www.diabetesportal.com/teentalk/articles/jdrf.htm (accessed September 12, 2005).

18. See www.abcnews.go.com/sections/politics/DailyNews/poll010626.html (accessed September 12, 2005).

19. Posted on *DiaryProject.com*, March 23, 2005. www.diaryproject.com/entries/?84006 (accessed September 14, 2005).

4 Religious Restrictions and Protections

> **As a Wiccan, I see a lot of discrimination . . . religious discrimination [against Wiccans].—Rachel, teen writer, Student Center Network[1]**

When religious principles or spiritual traditions collide with local, state, or federal laws, people may face a choice: to live according to their convictions or to deny their beliefs and comply with the law. In some instances, a court may place limits on a religious practice because it does not conform to community standards or is a threat to public health and safety. A court may also allow an exemption to a law in order to provide for free exercise of a religious or spiritual practice. In addition, courts may intervene when individuals or groups file lawsuits charging religious discrimination.

RESTRICTIONS ON RELIGIOUS PRACTICES

An early and classic example of government restriction of a religious practice is the ban against polygamy (having more than one marriage partner), as practiced in the nineteenth century by the Church of Jesus Christ of Latter-Day Saints, or Mormons. Many Mormons had settled in Utah (which had not yet become a state), where they could live by their belief that men should have multiple wives. But in 1862, the U.S. Congress

EXCOMMUNICATING MORMON TEENS

Although polygamy is no longer part of Mormon church doctrine, a small sect called the Fundamentalist Church of Jesus Christ of Latter-Day Saints (FLDS) has defied the law banning plural marriages. Under the leadership of Warren Jeffs, an estimated ten thousand Latter-Day Saint members live in communities on the Arizona-Utah border. According to an Associated Press report, former church members, including teens who have been banned or have run away from the church, accuse Jeffs of brainwashing and of dominating every aspect of members' lives. The church not only arranges marriages but may order wives to leave their husbands and be reassigned to different men. Movies, television, and sports such as basketball and football are forbidden, and education seldom goes beyond eighth grade.

"We're taught the only way into heaven is through this church," teen Tom Sam Steed told a reporter. Steed is among an estimated four hundred excommunicated teens who "can't return to their families because church members are forbidden from associating with apostates [those who revolt against the faith]." Some teens have been kicked out of the church for "minor infractions such as watching a movie or talking to a girl."

When forced out of the community, teens for the most part have to survive on their own, although some have received help from former Latter-Day Saint members. One former member believes that the teens are being forced to leave because of the shortage of women for multiple marriages. In his opinion, "the older men don't want to compete with the young bucks. Sheer math will tell you a certain amount of them have to go."[2]

passed a law prohibiting this kind of marriage.

For some time, though, Mormons continued to live by their church doctrine, and dozens of men were jailed and convicted of violating federal law. One man appealed his guilty verdict, but in 1878 the U.S. Supreme Court upheld his conviction, with the chief justice at the time declaring that people in Western nations considered polygamy "odious." The justices proclaimed that polygamy was a social practice, not a religious one; thus, it was subject to legal bans.

By the 1890s Utah applied for statehood but was not allowed to join the union until it denounced polygamy. Mormon leaders agreed that multiple marriage partners would no longer be sanctioned by the church; as a result, Congress voted to admit Utah as a state. In short, the federal government was able to force Mormons to live by mainstream religious values.

Other types of restrictions on the free exercise of religion may occur when community authorities believe that they must protect lives, such as by barring a church from using poisonous rattlesnakes and copperheads in religious services. While this practice is not widespread, some Pentecostal churches in states such as Tennessee, Kentucky, and Virginia believe that they should follow biblical instructions in Mark 16:17–18: "And these signs shall follow them that believe; In my name shall they cast out devils; they shall speak with new tongues; They shall take up serpents; and if they drink any deadly thing, it shall not hurt them; they shall lay hands on the sick, and they shall recover." Church members who "take up serpents" say they are obeying God. Although serpent handling is outlawed in some Southern states, the ban is not easily enforced because of the First Amendment right to the free exercise of religion. Even though a person may be endangering his or her life, the act is voluntary. Indeed in 2004, a preacher in Virginia was bitten by a rattlesnake that he was handling during an Easter service; he refused medical treatment and died, which many members believed was God's will.

Other limits on religious practices include forcing people to undergo medical procedures that are against their religious doctrines. One example involves a court ruling that a person should undergo drug treatments for cancer in spite of her or his objections on religious grounds. Or a hospital might order blood transfusions for children or adults whose religion prohibits this procedure, such as Jehovah's Witnesses. One teenage girl who is a Jehovah's Witness described how she felt when she was forced to undergo a blood transfusion: "It's no different than somebody getting sexually assaulted or raped or robbed or something. You'd feel violated because it's not anybody else's property, it's you."[3]

Some state courts have ruled that parents who refuse medical treatment should be forced to have their children vaccinated against contagious diseases such as measles and whooping cough. In fact, most states have laws requiring vaccinations before children begin attending school. However, nearly all states—excluding Arkansas, Mississippi, and West Virginia—allow religious exemptions for parents who, based on their faith, do not want their children inoculated. The American Medical Association and many public health officials

What's Your Opinion?

A majority of Americans, including many legal experts, contend that faith healing can result in sacrificing children for religious beliefs. But those who sincerely practice spiritual healing believe that they are acting according to their conscience and are being responsible parents. So questions arise: Is it a government's responsibility to force parents to rely on medical technology? Some people have been seriously injured or have died under the care of highly competent physicians. When parents believe that prayer heals and is a life-saving measure, are they justified in relying solely on prayer? What's your opinion?

oppose these exemptions, arguing that without vaccinations there is increased risk of national epidemics.[4]

PLEDGE OF ALLEGIANCE

Decades ago, a religious exemption was at the heart of a U.S. Supreme Court case regarding the Pledge of Allegiance in public schools. Until the 1940s some state laws required all school children to take part in a ceremony pledging allegiance to the U.S. flag. But some religious denominations, such as Jehovah's Witnesses, some Mennonites, and other less-well-known groups, believe that the pledge ceremony is an offense against biblical laws. In their view, a compulsory flag salute violates First Amendment rights, and the U.S. Supreme Court agreed. In short, a mandatory pledge of allegiance was ruled unconstitutional.

Although no one can legally be compelled to recite the pledge, debates about its wording have been ongoing since

1954, when President Dwight Eisenhower approved the addition of the phrase *under God* after the word *nation* in the pledge. A majority of Americans believe that the phrase is appropriate. But many people, from atheists to varied religious groups, object to the *under God* phrase, claiming that it violates the establishment clause and should be removed.

In 2002, an atheist in California, Michael A. Newdow, objected to his daughter's having to recite the pledge in her school, and he filed a lawsuit against the school district. The case went all the way to the U.S. Supreme Court, but in 2004 the justices found that Newdow, who sees his daughter on weekends only, lacked legal standing to pursue the case. That is, because the girl's mother has custody of her, the father did not have the right to represent his daughter in regard to her education, medical care, or other issues.

Newdow, however, filed another lawsuit on behalf of three parents and their children (unnamed) who had the right to sue. A U.S. district judge in California heard the case and on September 14, 2005, ruled that the *under God* phrase violates the rights of children to be "free from a coercive requirement to affirm God." The judge issued a restraining order that prevents "the recitation of the pledge at the Elk Grove Unified, Rio Linda and Elverta Joint Elementary school districts in Sacramento County, where the plaintiffs' children attend," according to a news report.[5]

The decision could lead to another high court hearing, and it has triggered many public comments on the case. Even before the district court judge ruled, the pledge issue was frequently discussed in high schools and on teen Internet forums. Reacting to the Newdow case, a fourteen-year-old declared in a *Kidzworld.com* post,

> I think that there is absolutely no reason that the Pledge of Allegiance should be changed. Whether it was just changed to say "under God" in 1954 doesn't make a difference in whether it's a tradition or not. It's a tradition to me because I was not even alive in 1954 to know the other version. If Michael Newdow (or anyone else for that matter) is offended enough to take this case to the Supreme Court, then you would think that

> the school would excuse his daughter from saying the Pledge. In my opinion, America should not change a well-known tradition because one person disagrees. What will become of us then?[6]

In a feature on *ChannelOne.com* website, seventeen-year-old Marisa Berroteran notes, "I believe that the pledge of allegiance should continue to include 'One nation, under God'. . . . I don't see how that would offend anyone who doesn't like it because they can just choose not to say it." Paul Gessler, eighteen, objects: "I don't believe public school teachers should lead the pledge because they would be promoting Christianity as an employee of the state."[7]

SCHOOL ATTENDANCE

In most states, laws require students to attend school until the age of sixteen. But some religious groups known collectively as the Amish, or "plain people," believe that their faith requires them to live separately from the world and maintain a simple way of life, with plain dress and without modern conveniences or public schooling. The most conservative are the Old Order Amish, who use horses and buggies for transportation and have horse-drawn farm wagons, plows, and other equipment.

After attending a one-room school through eighth grade, Amish teens are expected to work on the family farm or in a family business, making furniture or buggies or operating a fabric shop. In years past, several states tried to force Amish youth to attend public schools until they reached sixteen years of age, but the U.S. Supreme Court in 1972 ruled that state compulsory education laws jeopardized the freedom of the Amish to live by their religious beliefs.

OTHER RELIGIOUS PROTECTIONS

After centuries of suppression and legal battles, Native Americans have won some exemptions for a traditional religious rite that dates back an estimated ten thousand years.

NOW YOU KNOW!

The Amish are Anabaptists, who stem from an old religious sect of sixteenth-century Europe and include Brethren, Hutterites, and Mennonites. Anabaptists of the past frequently debated the theology of the Catholic and Protestant churches in Europe. They set themselves apart from everything worldly, believing that they should live much as Christians did during the first century.

The Amish follow a simple, agrarian lifestyle, which they believe keeps them close to God.

Divisions eventually occurred among the Anabaptists, and some broke away to follow Jakob Ammann (or Jacob Amen), from whom the Amish took their name. Ammann believed in strict religious practices and a simple lifestyle. When they emigrated from Europe to North America, the Amish would not accept new technology as it developed, and they maintained their belief that worldly conveniences such as electricity and farm machinery would prevent them from being close to nature, where they could feel the presence of God.

Among the Anabaptists today, the Old Order Amish maintain a more rigid separation from U.S. society than do most of the other groups, although the Hutterites, most of whom are in Canada and the western United States, have separate communities also. Yet, not all of these communities farm full-time, because the cost of farming prevents many families from making a living. Some have had to turn to other occupations, such as carpentry, factory work in mobile home industries, and other construction.

How do Amish teens view their religious background and lifestyle? Most—about 90 percent—stay with the church and become part of the community.[8] Consider Jason, whose family is Old Order Amish in Geauga County, Ohio. At age sixteen, Jason received a buggy from his parents and took a job as a carpenter. As is customary, he turned his paycheck over to his father, who in turn gave Jason a $30 allowance for the week. He still followed that practice at age nineteen, when he was interviewed by a *Toledo Blade* reporter. Jason used some of the allowance to pay his admission to a game room where, with his friends, he could watch baseball on television, rent a movie, shoot pool, or read a newspaper, all of which the Amish religion forbids. While many Amish parents do not approve of this behavior, they tolerate it because "they know there ain't no use getting mad about it," Jason told a reporter. Parents reason, "If you just leave [young people] alone, they'll grow up." As Jason put it, "I'm glad I was born Amish, I'll tell you that. It's easier to be in the faith." He pointed out that teens may be wild for a while, "but they settle down when they join the church."[9]

The tradition involves the use of a controlled substance—a narcotic drug called peyote—in the Native American Church, which combines Christian and Native spiritual practices. Also known as the Peyote religion, the Native American Church conducts ceremonies in which peyote is consumed as a sacrament similar to taking communion in a Catholic or Protestant church. Using peyote for nonreligious purposes is considered sacrilegious and is illegal in the United States.

Peyote comes from the mushroomlike buttons atop a cactus found in Southwestern United States and Mexico. The buttons are dried and either chewed as food or brewed as tea. In a ceremony that lasts from sundown Saturday to sunrise Sunday, members of the Native American Church use peyote and, depending on individual reactions, may have visions or hallucinations, said to create oneness with the Creator, unity with ancestors, and a bond with other members of the group.

In spite of numerous efforts to ban peyote ceremonies, the right to practice the peyote sacrament was finally established in 1978, with passage of the American Indian Religious Freedom Act. The law says that "it shall be the policy of the United States to protect and preserve for American Indians their inherent right of freedom to believe, express, and exercise the traditional religions of the American Indian, Eskimo, Aleut, and Native Hawaiians, including but not limited to access to sites, use and possession of sacred objects, and the freedom to worship through ceremonials and traditional rites." Nevertheless, legal challenges have continued, and courts have ruled both against and in favor of peyotism.

In 1988, for example, two Native American men in Oregon were fired from their jobs because they took part in peyote rituals. A state law in Oregon had banned the use of peyote. The men sought state unemployment benefits but were denied, so they appealed their cases to the U.S. Supreme Court. The high court ruled in 1990 (*Employment Division, Department of Human Resources of Oregon, et al. v. Smith, et al.*) that a person's religious beliefs did not excuse him from complying with a valid state law. However, the ruling was overturned when the U.S. Congress passed a 1994 amendment to the

American Indian Religious Freedom Act. The amendment allows and protects the traditional use of peyote for religious purposes.

Sikh men wear a turban and grow a beard as part of their religious practices.

As the U.S. population has included evermore people of diverse religious beliefs, issues regarding the protection of religious practices in schools and the workplace have escalated in the past decade. For example, hairstyles and head coverings have become an issue for people faithful to their religious traditions. In a 2004 controversy at a California high school, a senior, who is a Sikh (pronounced *se-ikh*), was told by school authorities that he could not attend graduation ceremonies unless he removed his turban and wore a school cap. The student refused because the turban is a religious obligation, and after intervention from Sikh activists who cited civil rights laws against religious discrimination, school administrators allowed the student to wear his turban for the ceremonies.

In a workplace debate, two Sikh men were involved in another conflict over wearing turbans. Amric Singh and Jasjit Singh were hired in 2001 as traffic cops with the New York City Police Department (NYPD). This began a three-year fight for their right to wear turbans and to keep their uncut beards. In the Sikh religious tradition, men usually wear a peaked turban, known as the *dastaar*, to cover their long hair, which is never cut because it shows respect for what God has created. In addition, a devoted Sikh will not cut his beard and may twist his long facial hair and tuck it up into his turban.

After being hired by the NYPD, Amric Singh refused to comply with an order to trim his beard and remove his turban and was fired from his job. Jasjit Singh attempted to wear a police hat as ordered but soon felt that his rights were being denied, and he resigned from the police force. Both men filed

SIKHISM

Sikhs worldwide total eighteen million or more, but in the United States they are a relatively small group, with an estimated population of 190,000 to 440,000. But because of some of their religious attire and traditions, they have been targets of discrimination.

The turban has been part of the Sikh tradition ever since the founding of the religion, in the Punjab region of India, now Pakistan, during the late fifteenth century. According to Sikh beliefs, Shri Guru Nanak Dev Ji, born in 1469, was chosen by God to embody the Divine Light. He and the nine gurus who followed him wore turbans, and today the head coverings show commitment to the gurus, who are not worshipped but are regarded as teachers or prophets of the religion.

Other religious items that many Sikhs wear symbolize their unified community and are known as the five *Ks* because they begin with the letter *k* in the Punjabi alphabet. The five *Ks* are *kesh* (uncut hair), *kangha* (a wooden comb that symbolizes cleanliness), *kara* (a steel bracelet that says *Sikhs are servants of the Guru*), *kachh* (special underwear that reminds Sikhs to practice self-restraint over passions), and *kirpan* (a ceremonial religious sword symbolizing courage, dignity, self-reliance, and defense of the weak and oppressed).[10]

At Rutgers University in New Jersey, Sikh students have established a Sikh club that helps educate others on campus about their religion and reduces stereotypes and misconceptions. Sikh students frequently have to explain that they are not Hindus or Muslims and that "Sikhism is more of a way of life than the way that most people view a religion. It's the way that you should live your life," the club's president, Divnain Malik, explained. "You live your life true and pure and you'll reach God. The ultimate goal is to become one with God, to reach God. It teaches us to be true to ourselves."[11]

lawsuits charging that the NYPD's rule against turbans and beards violated city, state, and federal laws that prohibit religious discrimination. It was not until the end of July 2004 that the NYPD reversed its ban and allowed the two men to return to duty wearing their turbans and beards according to their religious faith.

Other religious discrimination issues may involve observing holy days that are not part of the dominant Christian faith. Most Christians worship on Sundays or observe religious holidays, such as Christmas, when many businesses are closed. But what about those religious groups whose Sabbath or holy days fall on regular workdays? Are employers required by law to allow workers days off for such observances as a Saturday Sabbath or religious holidays such as Diwali, the Hindu festival of lights; Yom Kippur, the Jewish Day of Atonement; the Buddhist new year; or Eid ul-Fitr, which ends a month of fasting for Muslims?

The Civil Rights Act of 1964 is the key federal law prohibiting discrimination. Title VII of the act requires that employers reasonably accommodate the religious needs of employees, such as holidays or Sabbath observances that do not occur on Sunday. However, this accommodation cannot place an undue burden on the employer. In some instances the "undue burden" provision applies to workers whose religion requires prayer breaks during the workday. An employer may reasonably expect a worker to make up the break time with a shorter lunch period or longer shift on the job.

The Civil Rights Division of the U.S. Department of Justice enforces federal statutes that prohibit discrimination based on religion in education, employment, housing, public accommodations, and access to public facilities. The department has published a brochure that provides an introduction to the laws against religious discrimination. Posted on the Internet, the brochure also explains how to report claims to the various sections of the Civil Rights Division and tells where to find out more about one's rights.[12]

NOTES

1. Rachel, "Right and Wrong: Religious Discrimination," *Studentcenter.org*, September 2004. http://articles.studentcenter.org/index/173 (accessed October 20, 2004).
2. Quoted in Associated Press, "Polygamous Church Kicks Out Hundreds of Boys," *St. Petersburg Times*, September 5, 2004, 5A.
3. Quoted in an Internet forum post, "14-Year-Old Jehovah's Witness Forced by Court to Accept Transfusion," *Rabble.ca*, April 12, 2005. www.rabble.ca/babble/ultimatebb.php?ubb=get_topic&f=21&t=001173 (accessed September 13, 2005).
4. Donald G. Mcneil Jr., "Worship Optional: Joining a Church to Evade Vaccine," *New York Times*, January 14, 2003. www.nytimes.com.
5. David Kravets and the Associated Press, "Judge: School Pledge Is Unconstitutional," *Chicago Tribune*, September 15, 2005. www.chicagotribune.com.
6. Cyberchic02, "Pledge of Allegiance Feedback," *Kidzworld.com*. www.kidzworld.com/site/p2270.htm (accessed September 10, 2005).

7. Quoted in Nikki I., "Under God?" *ChannelOne.com*. www.channelone.com/news/exchange/news/2003/10/24/se_under/ (accessed October 4, 2004).

8. Joe Militia, "Amish Roll with Change," *Washington Times*, May 11, 2004. www.washtimes.com.

9. Quoted in Dee Drumond, "Teenagers Stray, but Usually Find Their Way Back," *Toledo Blade*, May 7, 2001. http://toledoblade.com/apps/pbcs.dll/article?AID=/20010507/SRAMISH/105070014 (accessed September 13, 2005).

10. "Sikhs at the Crossroads," *Religionwriters.com*, September 8, 2004. www.religionwriters.com/public/tips/080904/080904b.shtml (accessed October 18, 2004); also see, B. A. Robinson, "Sikhism," *ReligiousTolerance.org*, March 16, 2004. www.religioustolerance.org/sikhism.htm (accessed October 18, 2004); Robert Pollack, *The Everything World Religions Book* (Avon, MA: Adams Media, 2002), 184.

11. Quoted in Agatha E. Rubins, "RU Sikh Tries to Erase Stereotypes, Ignorance," *Daily Targum*, April 24, 2005. www.dailytargum.com/news/2005/04/24/University/Ru.Sikh.Tries.To.Erase.Stereotypes.Ignorance-935873.shtml?page=1 (accessed May 6, 2005).

12. U.S. Department of Justice, *Protecting the Religious Freedom of All Americans: Federal Laws against Religious Discrimination*. www.usdoj.gov/crt (accessed October 19, 2004).

Religion in Everyday Life

Are teens more or less religious than their parents? What do teens believe? How do teens practice their religion? Do most teens define themselves by their religion? Do most teens believe in God? These are just a few of the questions that youth have answered in surveys over the past few years.

Every day, before I go to breakfast, I walk outside into the cool morning air and pray to the Creator. My elders say that we must respect life because everything in this world contains a life force. They say to put out tobacco every morning in appreciation for each new day . . . and for the gifts that the Great Spirit has given each of us. —Clarence D. Meat Jr., Cheyenne and Arapaho Tribes of Oklahoma, written at age seventeen[1]

The National Study of Youth and Religion, led by sociologist Christian Smith at the University of North Carolina, Chapel Hill, surveyed more than thirty-three hundred teens aged thirteen to seventeen and found that 80 percent believe in God. In addition, most teens follow the religious practices of their parents. For example, 86 percent of conservative Protestant teens and 75 percent of Jewish teens report that they practice their parents' religion. Findings from this study were published in 2005 in *Soul Searching: The Religious and Spiritual Lives of American Teenagers* by Smith and coauthor Melinda Lundquist Denton.

However, few youth in the study could actually articulate the basic doctrines of their religion. For many of the participants, God exists and created the world. "God wants people to be good, nice, and fair to each other," teens say. According to Smith, teens believe that "the central goal of life is to be happy and feel good about oneself. God does not need to be particularly involved in one's life except when God is needed to resolve a problem. Good people go to heaven when they die." One seventeen-year-old Mormon in the study appeared to sum up this view in an interview: "I believe in, well, my whole religion is where you try to be good and, ah, if you're not good then you should just try to get better, that's all."[2]

The study by Reboot also inquired about teens' religious beliefs and found that many "attend worship services on a regular basis," but "just as many others—if not more—practice their faith informally." In the survey, 44 percent of respondents said that they were "religious," and 35 percent called themselves "spiritual but not religious." Some youth simply believe it is possible to be religious or spiritual without belonging to a church, synagogue, or mosque. According to the study, youth

> find their way to religious expression by spending time with their friends in informal group settings. There is a genuine attachment to religious life and very little loss of faith, but it occurs in the context of a full life complete with competing worries about getting good grades, finding a job or getting a sexually transmitted disease. Moreover, it takes place as young people are integrated into diverse networks with people of many religious persuasions and backgrounds.[3]

SPEAKING OUT ABOUT RELIGION

While some teens may be vague about what they believe, many youth do speak out clearly about how their religion influences them. Sarah Flam, for example, belongs to a Jewish temple in southern California. She says that her religion "affects my morals and the way I act in my life." She explains that people have beliefs different from hers, which often reflects on her relationship with others, because people don't understand her religion. But that, she says, "makes me want to stand up for what I believe in [even] more."

Two other teens at the same temple also say that they have a personal set of morals gained through their religion. One young man noted that Judaism has a "very big impact" on his everyday life, and he often thinks about whether his actions are right according to the Torah.

Mansoor Siddeeq, seventeen, a member of Nur-Allah Islamic Center in Indianapolis, Indiana, notes, "My faith is the first priority in my life. I was taught since I was little that religion comes first."[4]

In Tallahassee, Florida, Hailey Bevis wears a T-shirt printed with bold letters that read, "Jesus is my homeboy." Bevis is like many other teens and adults across the United States who want to proclaim their Christian faith. Some opt for the shirt with the statement "Mary is my homegirl." A Kansas teen says, "It's really cool that people are able to wear those shirts and not be criticized. But I don't like it when people wear them and say they are all into God and then they don't walk the talk, they're just about the trend. I really respect it and think it's cool when they wear it and are really representing their faith."[5]

In Arizona, New Mexico, and other Western states, young and old alike buy *milagros* (Spanish for "miracles"), talismans, or charms said to have supernatural powers and used as prayer aides—to petition for good health, safety, and protection for oneself, family members, friends, property, and animals. They stem from an ancient Hispanic tradition traced back to the Iberians who lived along the Spanish coast several centuries before Christ.

Today, the charms are made of metal, wood, wax, clay, or other materials and may be shaped like body parts—a foot, ear, heart, hand—or animals; they are offered to a saint for healing or thanks for an answered prayer. The *milagros* are often attached to statues of Catholic saints or to the walls of churches and may be components of jewelry. At a shop called Suenos Latin American Imports, in Phoenix, Arizona, customers

CHECK IT OUT!

The novel *Katelyn's Affection*, by Kirsten Klassen, focuses on a teen from a Mennonite background who, like many teens, is searching for meaning in her life. Katelyn is dealing with two church-going parents who are divorcing, a situation that makes her question whether she's ready to make a commitment—either to her Mennonite boyfriend who's away at college or to her non-Mennonite boyfriend who seems to understand her so well.

Mennonites are known for their pacifist views, and Katelyn's spiritual crisis in the book hinges on this, not as a reader might expect on opposition to war, but instead on her reaction to Leah's, her best friend's, abusive boyfriend. Katelyn is seized by a desire for revenge that shocks her and makes her feel unworthy to be a Mennonite. Nonviolence is one of the cornerstones of her religion that she believes in deeply. Her non-Mennonite boyfriend understands and appreciates how she is torn between what she believes is right and what she wants to do. He shows her that a desire to get even is not the same as actually taking action.

***Katelyn's Affection* deals with questions about some of the choices teens may have to make in their lives, such as, How do you help a friend who is in trouble? How do you accept divorce without blaming one of the parents? How can you be faithful to your religious beliefs in the face of emotional contradictions? But the book does not provide tidy answers. As the author points out, "I wanted to raise questions in my book but not shove answers down readers' throats. Teens should have the opportunity to sort their convictions out for themselves."[6]**

include Hispanics, Anglo-Americans, teens of various cultural backgrounds, members of the U.S. Marines, pagans, devout Catholics, and others who believe in miracles and the protective power of *milagros*.[7]

IN PRINT, ON THE NET

In recent years, teen religious views have appeared increasingly in print and electronic media. For example, a Muslim teen, Eba Hamid, wrote for Knight-Ridder news,

> I don't go around preaching my religion to my friends, but they know what I believe in and they accept me. When I go out with them, I pay attention to the food I eat. I check everything I order to make sure there is no bacon, ham or anything made of pork. When a few of them started experimenting with drugs

> and alcohol, I never even thought of joining in. Through my religion, I was raised to believe those things are damaging, and I never messed with them.[8]

In 2004, *Seventeen* magazine and its companion website carried a variety of comments from teens about faith issues. In one section, teens answered the question "Do you believe in God?" Responses ranged from true believers to agnostics. A sixteen-year-old wrote, "I believe in God with all my heart, mind, and soul. . . . Everything I do is based on my belief," while a seventeen-year-old stated simply, "I don't believe in any higher power."[9]

Teen expressions about their religious beliefs have been posted on the website for *Kiwibox.com*, an online magazine. In one posting, Amy wrote about being a Bahá'í and said that she is often asked what Bahá'ís believe. "Well, we believe that there is one God and that mankind is one. We believe in the equality of men and women, we believe in the elimination of prejudices of all kinds. Sound kind of familiar? I think all good people believe these things."[10]

A section of a website for Palo Alto High School (California) called *Paly Voice* shows how religion or lack of it plays a role among the students. Posting articles from its student magazine *Verde*, the site gives voice to atheist, Catholic, Hindu, Jehovah's Witness, Mormon, and United Methodist students. For example, Alberto Prado is a Jehovah's Witness and explained that he goes with a group "door to door to distribute publications related to the Bible." They hand out a Witness magazine, *Watchtower* or *Awake*, and ask, "Do you read the Bible? This magazine helps extract lessons from the Bible and relate them to real life." If asked, Prado or any other member of the faith tells listeners that Jehovah's Witnesses do not celebrate birthdays or holidays, do not salute or pledge allegiance to any flag, and do not allow blood transfusions—practices that they believe are an offense against biblical laws.

How does Prado apply his faith to everyday life? "I would not be where I am now without my religion because I would not have a reason to do anything," he told a *Verde* magazine reporter. "Since I know that all will be well some day, I just never let anything get to me too much." His religion gives him hope that "we can indeed live life on Earth in a good way. God can take an active part in everyone's life."[11]

Another posting on the same *Paly* website describes how Hinduism guides student Karishma Oza, who among other practices prays each night to the gods and goddesses (manifestations of the Infinite God), whose likenesses are in a *mandir*, or shrine, in her home. While she goes to a Hindu temple to pray when possible, that does not determine whether she is a faithful Hindu. "You don't have to go to temple to be Hindu. . . . You don't have to do anything except believe in the values and worship." The values she refers to are doing good to others and treating them well, respecting everyone, and doing the right thing. "Hinduism helped me determine my morals,"

Check It Out!

"My everyday life is totally affected by Buddhism. It has to be. The 4 Noble Truths run my life. Buddhism isn't just a religion. It's a way of life."[12] *Buddha in Your Backpack: Everyday Buddhism for Teens*, by Franz Metcalf. The book is divided into three parts, with the first telling about the life of Buddha, a word from a Sanskrit/Pali that means "one who has awakened or been enlightened." The second part of the book applies Buddhist wisdom to teen life, and the third, called "Taking a Buddhist Path," is what the author describes as "the classic metaphor for Buddhism. The Buddha saw life as a path. . . . The path has no end, so what matters is simply taking steps along it." Included also are instructions on how to meditate, "a traditional Buddhist practice to help your body and mind, regardless of your religious beliefs."[13]

A VOICE FROM A RELIGIOUS COMMUNE

One section of a website for the Bruderhof Community focuses on teens' views. The Bruderhof is an international network of religious communal settlements dedicated to nonviolence, simplicity, and service. In the United States, Bruderhof communities can be found in New York and Pennsylvania, and daily life varies with each community, but "most have the same basic schedule and departments, including a nursery, kindergarten, and elementary school, a communal kitchen and laundry, and various workshops and offices." Families have their own apartments and share their noon and evening meals in a communal dining room. "Dinner is typically followed by a meeting for prayer, sharing, and decision making, or simply for singing."[14] People in the community wear modest clothing—women and girls, for example, wear long skirts and head scarves. On the "Teen Voices" section of the site, sixteen-year-old Hannah Sorensen from a Bruderhof Community describes her experiences in a school far from her home and what she learned about her faith:

> Half way through the school year, my family went to Minnesota for a long-term visit with my grandparents. During our stay, I attended the Minnesota Business Academy in St. Paul, where I was the only student from the Bruderhof.
>
> On my first day at the school, I was a nervous wreck, paranoid of getting teased and worried that I would be ignored and shunned. I was exceedingly embarrassed when classmates started asking me why I wore long skirts and if I always covered my head with a scarf.
>
> Nevertheless, I pulled myself together and did my best to answer their questions. Soon, I realized that these people were not trying to torment me as I had previously imagined. They were sincerely interested in the person underneath the plaid dress. Once I had made this discovery, my embarrassment evaporated; after a couple of weeks, I felt totally accepted and at home.
>
> The friendly interest of my classmates helped me to sort out my own beliefs, opinions, and faith. Questions I had heard repeated themselves inside me; sometimes followed by answers, sometimes not. What do I actually believe in? Do I wear these clothes just because I grew up on the Bruderhof, or do I really believe I should? Would I rather dress like "normal" or average people? Not only did my time at MBA help me to define myself; I also got to know a wonderful rainbow of people, each one unique.

Statues of Buddha take many forms, but this smiling, sitting Buddha is a common one.

she explains in the article posting. "It helped me learn to do what's right in life and to choose things for myself."[15]

In their everyday lives, some teens say they have serious conflicts with religious beliefs. As Leslie Leahy, an Indiana teen, put it, "I have been to many different churches and all seem like they are forcing their beliefs on you and if you don't believe in them you are not a good person. I can not and will not be forced to believe in something if it feels wrong."[16]

A seventeen-year-old in a post on the website *DiaryProject.com* wrote that she also has "been to many different churches, christian, catholic, and a buddist temple as well as others." She wonders, "Why do people pray? You don't know whom you are praying to, you just have an idea from peoples beliefs . . . you never know what's true."[17]

On the same website, an eighteen-year-old girl poses a question that many ask: "how do you guys KNOW god exists? it's like believing there's an orange behind a bush without being able to see it. i desperately want to believe in something, but nothing fits."[18]

HOLY DAYS

Although not an everyday event, various religious rituals and ceremonies honor specific holy days, or holidays, throughout a given year. The Sabbath, for example, is a day of worship—from sunset Friday to sunset on Saturday for Jews and Seventh-Day Adventists and Sunday for most Christians. Some of the most sacred holidays include Christian Easter (Jesus's rising from the dead); the ten-day Jewish holidays beginning with Rosh Hashanah (Jewish New Year) and later Yom Kippur (Day of Atonement, marked by fasting, repenting, and praying); Muslim month of Ramadan (fasting, prayer, and meditation from sunrise to sundown each day of this sacred month).

For many young Americans, a holiday observance is a way to be connected to a community. Consider events on the Cornell University campus, where the Hindu Student Council holds "weekly bhajan [prayer song] sessions, and larger pujas [prayer ceremonies] to celebrate many of the significant religious holidays," according to Riti Singh, president of the council. These celebrations originated in India, as did the colorful Holi, a centuries-old commemoration of the god Vishnu's victory over a demon king. The council sponsors an annual Holi on campus as part of an effort to help non-Indians learn about the Hindu community and Indian culture. While there are religious elements, the holiday celebrates equality, and people from varied social and economic backgrounds get together and spread or throw handfuls of colored powder called *gulal* on each other, all in a festive spirit. People leave "happy and covered in color," Singh noted.[19]

Hanukah (Chanukkah), the festival of lights in Judaism, is another holiday that focuses on community. It frequently occurs about the same time as the Christmas celebration and is often mistakenly called a "Jewish Christmas" or an alternative to Christmas, but such is not the case. Hanukkah commemorates the victory of ancient Jews over the Syrians who

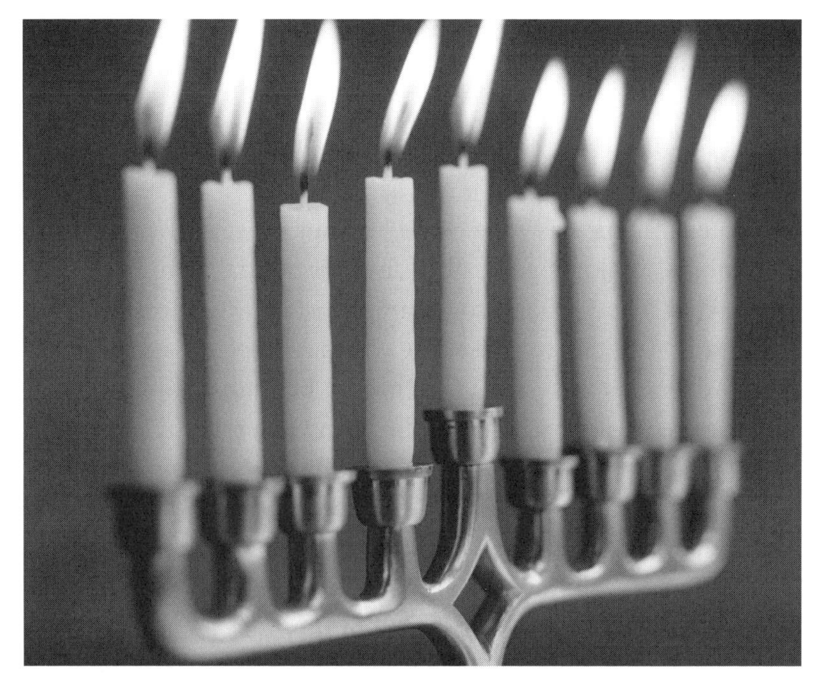

A menorah with its eight candles symbolizes Hanukkah.

ruled Israel at the time and defiled the Jewish temple. When Jews went to cleanse the house of worship and light the temple's lamp, there was only enough oil for one day, but miraculously the lamp stayed lit for eight days. Today, the menorah with its eight candles symbolizes the event.

Although Hanukkah is not a major religious observance like Rosh Hashanah and Yom Kippur, it is an important celebration for many Jewish youth, especially those living in communities that are predominantly Christian. For instance, two teens, Lisa and David Ginsburg, at Wausau West High School (Wisconsin) commemorate Hanukkah but not Christmas, which everyone else in the school celebrates. As Lisa noted, "Hanukkah and being Jewish, it is such an integral part of me." The holiday connects her to her roots, and her brother David told a reporter that being Jewish "is a point of pride for me. It sets me apart."[20]

Among many Greek Orthodox Christians, community is also foremost in the celebration on January 6 of Epiphany, which commemorates the baptism of Jesus. In Tarpon Springs, Florida, for example, where many Greek immigrants settled, the annual Epiphany celebration is considered one of the most traditional and colorful in the United States. Thousands of people from diverse faiths and denominations witness the ceremony, which begins at St. Nicholas Cathedral with a Divine Liturgy service. Then the archbishop leads a procession to a body of water called the Spring Bayou, where after an invocation, a teenage girl releases a dove, and the archbishop casts a cross into the water. Nearly four dozen teenage boys dive in after it. When one of the divers comes up with the cross, he receives a blessing from the archbishop.

News reporters who have covered the event have sought comments from teenage girls about their roles. Many believe their secondary participation is as it should be. Why? "Because it's the church rules!" one teen said. Others noted, because "Christ was a male" (a boy when he was baptized). One seventeen-year-old declared that "women have always done other important roles in the church [and] we have to make the men feel important." Another commented, "I'd rather be a dove bearer. . . . I feel I got a blessing just to be able to hold the Holy Spirit in my hands."

Nevertheless, a few girls said they wanted to dive. "I think girls should have the right. I really don't like the fact that boys are the only ones. I feel strongly about it," one girl told a reporter. Her friend added, "Girls can do the same things guys can."[21]

Many adults, particularly staunch believers, are outraged that there is even talk about girls participating in the dive. In the view of several, the idea is an insult to the faith. Some argue that the Epiphany celebration is centuries old and has nothing to do with being politically correct—allowing rights to girls. The faithful insist that girls don't dive, because in the Greek Orthodox tradition that activity is for boys only. End of discussion.

EXPLOITATION OR SINCERE INTEREST?

In recent years, interest in Native American communities and spirituality has grown across the United States, and some New

Native Americans wear special regalia to perform sacred dances in a great variety of spiritual ceremonies.

Age groups and non-Native individuals have tried to incorporate tribal ceremonies into their daily lives. It's a practice that many Native people condemn. As teen Loretta Cajero noted in *Soaring Spirits*, a book of interviews with Native youth, "Outsiders come in to witness our ceremonies that used to be sacred. Then they start trying to market things that they have seen, like maybe photographs. They're trying to make a fast buck off our culture. And I do not like that! I don't like the Indian being exploited in any way!"[22]

In a commentary in the *People's Voice*, Pte Cante Winyan pointed out that

> it has now become fashionable to "be Indian." All over the country there are people claiming to be taught by, and in some cases, direct descendants of well-known American Indian

> leaders. These people are neither teachers in the old ways, taught by, descendants of, nor are they sanctioned by the Nations they claim to be part of. They are what is commonly called "wannabes." These are people who find a little of the ways, find unsuspecting future wannabes and form a "tribe." They then start to create their own brand of Indian teachings—taking from this one and then adding to it. Then they learn a little more and change it just slightly to fit their purpose, add a little teachings from other religions and the stage is set to go out and "teach" the people—but for money.[23]

Such exploitation is frequently found on the Internet, where there are numerous sites that attempt to explain Native American spirituality and practices—for a price. But some websites are truly authentic. Usually, you can evaluate this by determining whether:

- **home pages are monitored by Native organizations or tribes;**
- **an e-mail address is available to contact the person responsible for the website and to ask questions about the reliability of postings;**
- **a tribal leader endorses the site with a welcoming message or perhaps a statement of purpose;**

Now You Know!

Large numbers of teens who identify themselves as being religious and having access to the Internet visit religious websites, indicating that the web has become a significant place of religious connection for a sizable portion of religious U.S. teens. Among teens who say that religious faith is extremely important to them, 40 percent report visiting religious websites a few times each month or more often.[24]

What's Your Opinion?
Some people say that it's okay to share information about one's faith when asked, but they don't believe that they should try to convert anyone to their beliefs. Others contend that they are required by their faith to help people find "truths" that bring about positive changes in their lives. What's your opinion? If you have a strong religious faith, what would you do?

- **content is presented from a Native point of view, not from a non-Native telling about Indians; and**
- **information about Native spirituality is offered in a general way but does not propose to teach a religious practice for a price.**

Some books and magazines contain reliable information about Native beliefs, but these publications often focus on specific ceremonies or tribal practices. Only a few include the beliefs of Native American teens and young adults. One is *Seventh Native American Generation*, or *SNAG*, a magazine written and illustrated by Native American youth. The magazine features first-person essays, poetry, photographs, and illustrations created by Native youths throughout the United States and Canada.

NOTES

1. Clarence D. Meat Jr., "Holding On to the Past," in *Night Is Gone, Day Is Still Coming: Stories and Poems by American Indian Teens and Young Adults* (pp. 106–8), ed. Annette Pina Ochoa, Betsy Franco, and Traci L. Gourdine (Cambridge, MA: Candelwick Press, 2003), 106.
2. Quoted in Christian Smith, *Soul Searching: The Religious and Spiritual Lives of American Teenagers*, with Melinda Lundquist Denton (Oxford: Oxford University Press, 2005), 162–163.

3. Anna Greenberg, *OMG! How Generation Y Is Redefining Faith in the iPod Era* (New York: Reboot, 2005), 6, 10.

4. Quoted in John Shaughnessy, "Luring Teenagers to Religion," *Indianapolis Star*, September 26, 2004, on *ReligiousNewsBlog.com*. www.religionnewsblog.com/8843 (accessed May 1, 2005).

5. Quoted in Jenee Osterheldt, "What Would Jesus Wear?" *RecordNet.com*, September 11, 2004. http://online.recordnet.com/articlelink/091304/lifestyle/articles/091304-l-2.php (accessed February 6, 2006).

6. Kirsten Klausen, personal correspondence, December 31, 2005.

7. Dan Carlin, "Little Shop of Miracles," *Arizona Republic* (Phoenix), August 27, 2004, E1; see also, "Collecting Milagros," *Collector's Guide Online*. www.collectorsguide.com/fa/fa052.shtml (accessed September 21, 2004).

8. Eba Hamid, "I Am a Normal Teenager—with a Difference," Knight-Ridder/Tribune News Service, August 24, 2004, n.p.

9. Quoted in "Do You Believe in God?" *Seventeen*, August 2004, 123.

10. Amy J., "I'm a Bahá'í," March 27, 2005, *Kiwibox.com*, www.kiwibox.com/article.asp?a=33073 (accessed April 30, 2005).

11. Quoted in Rotem Ben-Schachar, "I Am a Jehovah's Witness," *Paly Voice*, February 28, 2005. http://voice.paly.net/view_story.php?id=2662 (accessed April 30, 2005).

12. Quoted in Franz Metcalf, *Buddha in Your Backpack: Everyday Buddhism for Teens* (Berkeley, CA: Seastone, 2003), 140.

13. Metcalf, *Buddha in Your Backpack*, xxi.

14. Bruderhof Communities, "Family Life." www.bruderhof.com/us/Who_we_are/FamilyLife.htm (accessed April 30, 2005).

15. Quoted in Becca Chacko, "I'm a Hindu," *Paly Voice*, February 10, 2005. http://voice.paly.net/view_story.php?id=2569 (accessed April 30, 2005).

16. Leslie Leahy, personal correspondence, November 2004.

17. Sayitisntso, "Confused," *DiaryProject.com*, February 10, 2005. www.diaryproject.com/entries/?83134 (accessed June 11, 2005).

18. Tinkerbell, "Is God Real?" *DiaryProject.com*, January 9, 2005. www.diaryproject.com/entries/?82400 (accessed June 11, 2005).

19. Quoted in Sanika Kulkarni, "C.U. Celebrates Holi," *Cornell Daily Sun*, April 25, 2005. www.cornellsun.com.

20. Quoted in Elizabeth Putnam, "Jewish Teens Celebrate Their Roots," *Daily Tribune*, December 7, 2004. www.wisinfo.com/dailytribune/wrdtlocal/282936060897721.shtml (access May 6, 2005).

21. Quoted in Kelly Virella, "Girls Eye Diving for Cross in Ceremony," *St. Petersburg Times*, January 7, 2004, 8.

22. Karen Gravelle, *Soaring Spirits: Conversations with Native American Teens* (Lincoln, NE: iUniverse, 2000), 96.

23. Pte Cante Winyan, "Selling American Indian Spirituality 'Cheating Us, Cheating Them,'" *People's Paths*, August 1, 2000. www.yvwiiusdinvnohii.net/News2000/0800/WC000801Commentary.htm (accessed June 10, 2005).

24. National Study of Youth and Religion, "The Internet: A Resource for Religious Teens," December 10, 2003. www.youthandreligion.org/news/2003-1210.html (accessed September 22, 2004).

6 Religious Rites of Passage

> **When I reached puberty, my mother gave me a necklace to honor the occasion. . . . At the time, I did not know . . . that what had just occurred was an abbreviated form of a [Hindu] ceremony called the *ritu kala samskara*.—Ramya Gopal[1]**

Nearly all religious organizations, some nonreligious groups, and Native American spiritual practitioners mark the important events in the lives of their communities: birth, coming of age, marriage, and death. Often called *rites of passage*, these rituals vary with religious and spiritual groups in the United States.

Rituals at the beginning of life are common in some religions. In traditional Judaism, for example, birth rituals for a baby boy take place on the eighth day, when he is circumcised—the foreskin of the penis is removed. A trained person known as a *mohel* performs the circumcision. Traditionally a *mohel* is male, but in the United States a few are female. A *mohel* also says a blessing, recalling the Covenant between God and Abraham (Genesis 17:10–14). At the same time, the infant boy is named. In the Jewish faith, a baby girl also is named on the eighth day of life. Circumcision is also a birth ritual among some Muslim groups. However, Muslim boys may be circumcised any time between seven days and twelve years old.

Some Christian churches practice the ritual of infant baptism, which symbolizes that the baby is part of the Christian community. In the Greek Orthodox Church, for example, baptism is required for entry into heaven, so babies are baptized as soon as possible in the event tragedy strikes and takes a child's life at an early age. Other denominations—usually Protestant—baptize only adults.

COMING OF AGE

Ramya Gopal's words at the beginning of this chapter refer to a Hindu coming-of-age ceremony, *ritu kala*, practiced in India and sometimes in the United States by families from India. As an American living in Detroit, Michigan, Gopal knew little about the ceremony, so she asked her grandmother to explain it. In an essay for *Beliefnet.com*, Gopal shared what she learned.

> Like the coming-of-age society balls of the Victorian Era in England, this *samskara* (sacrament) was supposed to commemorate a girl's formal initiation into adult society. Yet unlike those secular and social parties of England, it was also supposed to signify an important point in the spiritual development of a girl. In the not-so-distant past, Indian parents would often arrange for their daughter's marriage to occur a few years before she reached puberty. . . . After marriage, she would remain in her parent's home until puberty, learning of the household duties she would perform later as a mother and a wife. After puberty, she would move into the house of her in-laws, serve her husband and live the life for which she had been prepared. Hence, the ritu kala not only recognized a young girl's important physical and emotional transformations, it also indicated her readiness to take on a woman's responsibilities, often including starting a family of her own.
>
> Unlike most Hindu celebrations, only women are present at the ritu kala. During the ceremony, the girl is presented with her first sari while all the ladies present gather near, sing songs of praise and shower her with gifts. In some communities, green-colored presents are given to invite fertility. While this

> Hindu ceremony, as it is traditionally performed, is slowly disappearing in India, it seems to have barely gotten started here in the U.S.[2]

For Native Americans, ceremonies are essential to an individual's and a community's spiritual life. Among the many rites of passage are boys' and girls' puberty rites, which are sacred rituals that usually last for days and may involve isolation and fasting to celebrate the transition from adolescent to adult. Rachel Cushman, a sixteen-year-old Chinook girl, explained that the ceremony takes "place within four full moons of your first menstrual cycle. . . . When a woman comes of age in my tribe (we're from the Northwest Pacific Coast), she must go through the sacred ceremony of her people. The ceremony is what every young woman waits for because you're honored when you enter womanhood."

Taking part in the ceremony requires special regalia, and Rachel describes hers with pride:

> My dress and leggings were made of white deer hide and trade beads. Each bead was sewn individually in a beautiful pattern. Bright colors were used to make me look brilliant and show my love for the Earth. The hairpieces were made out of a hawk feather my grandfather had given me and two minks my mother gave me. Every piece of my regalia was given as a gift. It is known as "bad totem" to buy any of the body wear.
>
> When the time came, we traveled to the mouth of the Columbia River. Returning to the place of my people brought me joy. I love to be near the ocean because I am a person of the sea.

Rachel explained that the men of the tribe brought salmon, which would be smoked for the celebration later, but "once the ceremony began, no men could see me until four days had past. I began a number of tasks that cannot be told, because they're sacred and only for the women members of the tribe to know. Men of the tribe have their ceremony, and the women have theirs."[3]

The Corn Grinding Ceremony for a Hopi girl's coming of age is described in *Meet Mindy: A Native Girl from the*

Southwest, one of a series of books on young Native Americans today. As Mindy relates, the ceremony

> lasted five days and was held at my grandma's . . . house. My aunts and grandmother were there to encourage me, but I was left alone most of the time, quietly spending the first four days using the traditional . . . grinding stone, to crush the hard corn kernels into fine cornmeal. . . .
>
> During the four days, I wasn't allowed to eat any meat, salt, or fat, or to spend time with any male members of my family. On the fifth day, my aunts and grandmother taught me how to make . . . special breads made with Hopi blue cornmeal. My aunts and grandmother also spent time talking with me about what it means to be a mature young Hopi woman, my new responsibilities as a young adult member of my clan, and how I'll be expected to act.[4]

Coming-of-age ceremonies for young boys may include a vision quest, although the quest is not limited to the early teen years in a boy's life. During the vision quest, boys separate themselves from the community to fast and meditate. The goal is to receive a vision or guidance from a spirit who will be helpful throughout a lifetime.

When Ginew Benton prepared for his coming-of-age ceremony at the Shinnecock reservation near Southampton, New York, he selected two men to be his sponsors and guides. Ginew and his sponsors went to a sweat lodge in the woods for purification. While sweat lodges vary, they are usually small structures with a framework of saplings covered with canvas, animal hides, or blankets. In the center is a hollowed-out area for hot rocks that have been heated on a fire outside the structure. Water is poured on the rocks to create steam.

While in the sweat lodge Ginew fasted for two days and later described some of his experiences. During his fast, "a deer and her fawn stayed by me. They weren't afraid of me at all," he reported. "A butterfly visited me, too." He also had a vision of an old woman who "came and sang for me. Oh, and a cricket sang me to sleep."[5]

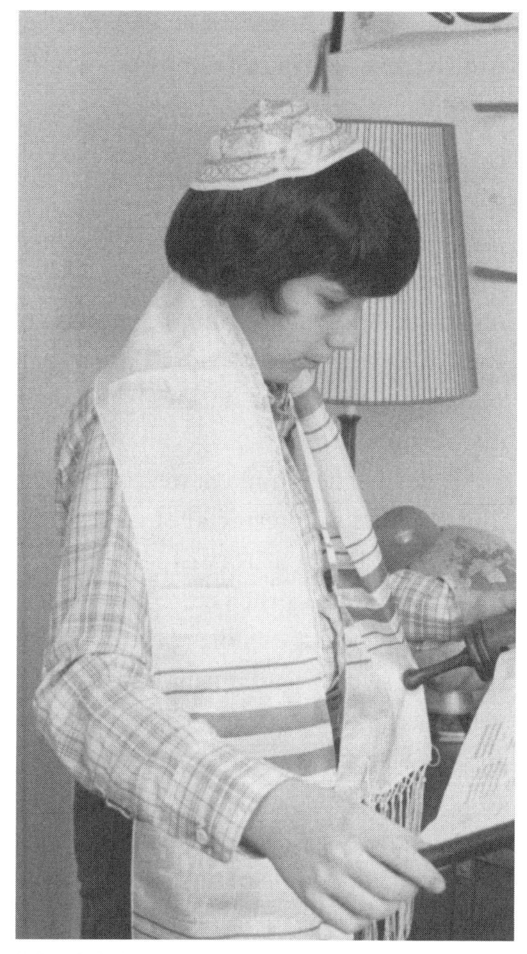
A Jewish boy demonstrates how he wore a yarmulke and prayer shawl and read from the Torah during his bar mitzvah ceremony.

After the sweat lodge, Ginew, like other Native Americans who take part in coming-of-age ceremonies, joined members of the reservation for a feast. Ginew had saved money to pay for the food, and he also had created gifts for his *give-away*, a part of the ceremony to show appreciation and emphasize the value of sharing.

Other coming-of-age ceremonies include a *bar mitzvah* (son of the commandment) in Judaism, which marks a Jewish boy's entry at age thirteen into the religious community as an adult. A *bat mitzvah* (daughter of the commandment), first introduced in the twentieth century, is the equivalent for girls, which may occur when they are as young as twelve years old. In Christian churches, a confirmation ceremony is common for youth who have studied their religion and confirmed their commitment to their faith. In turn, the congregation agrees to help them with their religious lives. *Rumspringa* is a coming-of-age tradition among Amish teens, who are allowed to vary from their religious rural lives and act as "typical" teens for a time, that is, wear jeans, go shopping in a mall, watch television, go to unsupervised parties, and even drink alcohol. Yet after their time of "rebellion" most Amish teens return to their families and church.

WEDDINGS

Weddings, of course, are rites of passage that indicate that two people are no longer single but have become a couple in marriage—both a civil and religious ceremony in most cases. But American wedding rituals are as varied as the religious (or nonreligious), ethnic, national, and racial backgrounds of the people involved.

Today in the United States, it is not unusual for couples to join together in interracial or interfaith marriages. But the nation has a long history of forbidding miscegenation, or racial mixing, in spite of the fact that the practice has existed since Europeans began exploring the continent and that it was certainly widespread during slavery. Many times over the centuries (and even now) Christians have declared that the Bible forbids mixing the races, using various biblical passages to "prove" their point, such as Genesis 11, in which God scatters the people of the earth. Antimiscegenists interpret this to mean that people of different nations should not marry. Yet, there is no reference to race anywhere in this or any other biblical verses cited.

It was not until 1967 that interracial marriages were officially sanctioned in the United States, with a Supreme Court decision in *Loving v. Virginia*. In 1958, Richard Loving and Mildred Jeter were married in Washington, D.C., because there was no waiting period before the ceremony could take place, which was not the case in their home state of Virginia. When the Lovings returned to their home, they were soon arrested for breaking the state's antimiscegenation law. They were each sentenced one year in jail, but the judge suspended the sentence on the condition they leave the state and not return for twenty-five years. Forced to move, they returned to Washington, D.C., where, in 1963, they initiated a lawsuit challenging the constitutionality of the antimiscegenation law. The Virginia Supreme Court of Appeals upheld the law, but in

June 1967, the U.S. Supreme Court unanimously ruled the law unconstitutional. Thus, in 1967, Virginia and other states that still had antimiscegenation laws on their books were forced to erase them. Since then interracial marriages have increased each year, as have interfaith and cross-cultural marriages, although there are no adequate statistics regarding these marriages.

Some religions do not allow interfaith marriages, so in such cases one of the partners may convert to the other partner's religion in order to be married in a religious ceremony. Or there might be two separate ceremonies, such as a Greek Orthodox wedding and a Hindu service. The Hindu partner may decide to be baptized in order to marry in the Greek Orthodox Church.

Some interfaith/intercultural weddings include a mix of religious traditions, as was the case with Ami Chen Mills, in San Francisco, California. Her marriage to "Barukh, a Sephardic Jew, was a blend of Jewish, Chinese, Christian and even Hawaiian traditions. Call it the melting pot of weddings," Mills wrote. She explained that

> a mixed wedding is a balancing act, but one with great rewards. . . . [It] is about unity, inclusion—and freedom. My fiancé and I included our ethnic and religious roots in our ceremony and reception, and enlisted family members from both sides to help. He and I chose what we loved about both of our cultures and family faiths, altered pieces and parts of tradition, and also rejected terminology and rituals we could not stand for.[6]

The rise in intercultural, interfaith, and interracial marriages has led to numerous websites and publications with advice both for and against such unions. Some sites and publications suggest how to plan interfaith weddings with a mixture of traditions and rituals.

Weddings, for example, may include traditional Christian wedding vows, a Jewish ritual of breaking glasses at the end of the ceremony, or the ritual of "Jumping the Broom," which is a tradition originating in Africa and is sometimes practiced by African Americans in honor of their ancestors and heritage. It symbolizes that a couple is entering a new life as husband and

Now You Know!
You've probably heard the saying that a bride should wear something old, something new, something borrowed, something blue, but does that relate in any way to a religious belief? The first three admonitions don't. Usually, something old is a personal gift from mother to daughter; a new item symbolizes the new family being formed; and a bride borrows something from a happily married woman in order to carry happiness into the new union. Wearing something blue, though, in Christian tradition symbolizes the purity of the Virgin Mary.

wife. It is also an ancient Celtic ritual used by some Pagans, who include Celtics, Druids, Wiccans, and others.

FUNERAL AND BURIAL CUSTOMS

For most young people, the teen years are the time when "real" life begins and death seems to be in the distant future; death and dying are seldom topics for discussion. Yet, by the end of their high school years, 20 percent of youth today "have experienced the death of a parent and out of 1,000 high school juniors and seniors, 90 percent have experienced the death of a loved one."[7] That means that many teens will likely attend a funeral—a rite of passage that marks the end of life.

Funerals include the rituals and etiquette that are observed before burial of the body or cremation of the deceased. Most funerals involve some type of ceremony, formal or informal, either steeped in religious tradition or specially created for the deceased and his or her loved ones. Traditional Protestant funerals, for example, are usually conducted by clergy in a church or chapel setting with a thirty- to sixty-minute program of prayers, hymns, eulogies, and, frequently, a sermon.

Funerals usually include burial rites—ritual practices conducted while placing the corpse in the ground after the service. Cremation is also a traditional practice in some religions, such as the Hindu, Buddhist, and Shinto faiths; a service may take place before or after cremation.

"In traditional Native American communities the ritual that occurs at death is very important," writes Terry Tafoya, a Native American *shaman* (spiritual leader). He cautions that practices differ in communities, but he describes the rites with which he is familiar—at the Warm Springs Indian Reservation, where his mother is on the tribal council. The rites begin with making deerskin clothing for the deceased because the deerskin decays "at the same rate as human flesh. It all goes back into the earth together." Embalming is not practiced, so spices are used to preserve the body, which is placed in a pine wood casket and is not buried for four days. "Our belief is that during the four-day ceremony the spirit of the person will retrace the steps he or she took in life," Tafoya explains. A give-away ceremony is part of the four-day event and involves giving away the deceased's belongings, "anything the dead person touched on a regular basis." A worship dance—a group dance with men on one side and women on the other—is actually the beginning of the funeral. Ceremonies with dancing may continue through a twenty-four- or forty-eight-hour period, although not everyone takes part throughout the night.[8]

While it may be customary in mainstream America for family and others who attend a funeral to wear dark clothing, white clothing is traditional at Muslim funerals. Funeral ceremonies usually involve readings, blessings, music, and eulogies—tributes to the deceased. Gifts of flowers or monetary donations to charities are frequently part of funerals, as are food and drink following burials.

Funeral rites for Roman Catholics include the vigil (or *wake*, as it's commonly known), the Funeral Mass, and the Rite of Committal, or burial in a Catholic cemetery. The wake usually takes place in a funeral home, family home, or parish church.

"WHEN I THINK OF DEATH . . . "

"When I think of death, I imagine a long journey from which one never returns," wrote teen Donia Regis in *Urban Health Chronicles.* Between her sixth and fifteenth years, she experienced numerous deaths. She explained:

> **Three of my friends were shot and killed, each a year apart. Three of my aunts died within that time period, each of natural causes. Of the six deaths, one was most devastating . . . the death of my great-aunt. . . . My family called her Granny. She was like a grandmother to everyone she knew and gave a helping hand whenever it was needed. Granny's funeral was the second funeral I attended. . . . My family told me that if I continued thinking about her she would always be a part of my life. But without her being here physically, things would never be the same. I had no one to turn to for answers about her death and no one to blame. So, I decided to blame God. I felt that someone as loving and caring as Granny did not deserve to be taken away from the people who loved her. Granny made a difference in my life.**
>
> **Because of her, I was able to go to church, get baptized and welcome God into my life. If she did this for Him, why did He take her away from her family?**

A year later, Donia was convinced that "even though it seemed unfair that God took Granny away, I no longer hold that against Him. It probably was time for her to join Him. I still miss Granny and pray that God will keep her face glowing in the sun and the stars until I see her again some day."[9]

The Funeral Mass is ordinarily the central element of Catholic funerals.

A traditional Jewish funeral is usually brief. Before the burial, there is no wake or visitation period, since viewing the body is considered disrespectful. A long-established custom among Orthodox Jews is for relatives of the deceased to tear their clothing as a sign of loss. Reform Jews, however, usually wear torn black ribbons given to them by the rabbi.

Among Jews—Reform, Conservative, and Orthodox—burial customs may differ. For example, Reform Jews may choose to have a body embalmed or cremated, which is not allowed in traditional Jewish burial customs because such practices are considered to be mutilation of the body. Traditional customs, which have survived for at least two millennia, require that the body be washed and wrapped in a simple white shroud, symbolizing that there is no distinction between rich and poor. Most communities have a Burial Society, an organization of volunteers who prepare a body for burial. Until after burial, the body is not left alone, and a group called *shomerim* sit with the deceased. Jewish law requires that the deceased be buried as soon as possible after death, which shows respect for the dead rather than worship of the deceased.

Muslims also follow the practice of covering a body in a shroud and burying the deceased soon after death occurs. The body is prepared for burial with a ritual washing performed by close family members who are the same gender as the deceased. Then the body is wrapped in a shroud and is traditionally placed in the ground without a casket, but that practice has changed somewhat in the United States. Now a body is usually placed in a coffin for burial.

At a Muslim funeral, the service is led by a close relative of the deceased, who stands by the head of a male body or by the trunk of a female corpse. Prayers are recited, and coffin bearers take the body to the grave site while repeating "God is great, God is merciful." After the body is lifted from the coffin and placed in the grave, close relatives enter the grave to loosen the shroud and turn the face toward Mecca. Each person in the funeral party puts three handfuls of dirt on the body and may also strew flowers or rose water that has been blessed.

AFTERLIFE BELIEFS

Most religious groups share the basic belief that the soul departs the body and, after judgment, may be destined for another type of passage—an afterlife, or eternal life, in a heaven or a hell. But there are numerous variations on the ways that Jews, Christians, Muslims, Hindus, Buddhists, and other religious groups perceive an afterlife. Teens, whatever their religious or spiritual background, express a variety of views, such as those in a documentary called *What Do You Believe?* by filmmaker Sarah Feinbloom. A Catholic teen responded to a question about possible consequences to him in the afterlife by saying "I'd rather do something on this earth that satisfies me as a person than go to Heaven."[10] On the website *Itsfinished.com*, teens had this to say:

> I don't believe people go to heaven or are reincarnated. They just die and that's it. But Nan was in pain and that means she is at total peace now.

> I believe in heaven, but I think people there can look down and keep an eye on us, and if we talk to them they can hear us.
>
> I believe that when some people die they stay around for a while as a spirit. My Dad died last year and I like to think that he is looking after me, like a guardian angel.
>
> I don't know about life after death but Mum lives on in our memories and thoughts and that's all I need to know.[11]

According to Orthodox Jewish beliefs, the dead will be resurrected when the Messiah appears, and there will be eternal life after death. Righteous souls meantime can enjoy a place similar to the Garden of Eden, and the wicked suffer in fiery pits. Some Conservative Jews believe that upon the coming of the Messiah, there will be physical life after death, while others contend that there is a spiritual afterlife in which the living sense and remember the deceased. On the other hand, Reform Jews and Reconstructionists reject the idea of life after death, believing that every soul is immortal and will eventually return to God or the universe.

Many Christian denominations believe in the second coming of Christ, which will be accompanied by the resurrection of the righteous (or believers in Jesus Christ). Faith in Jesus Christ and renouncing one's sins are essential if the resurrected soul is to achieve eternal life in heaven. Hell is reserved for those who do not accept Christ as their savior.

Unlike Protestant denominations, the Roman Catholic church believes there is a temporary place between heaven and hell called *purgatory*. Here souls may be tormented and purged of their sins and then ascend to heaven. The Greek Orthodox Church believes that the soul separates from the physical body immediately upon death and that a partial judgment begins regarding the character of person during his or her lifetime. This is considered a foretaste of heaven and hell.

The Quakers (Religious Society of Friends) is a Christian-like faith, but it has no religious dogma, and members have diverse attitudes about the possibility of an afterlife. Some

Friends are convinced that there is an afterlife, while others are sure there is not. Nearly all Quakers believe that speculations about the afterlife are not as important as attempts to improve the conditions of humanity in the present time. Some Quakers believe that whatever good or evil works people do in this life may go on in the lives of those of the next generations. Another view is that the human spirit survives and is a continuation of this life—perhaps moving ahead to more advanced states through reincarnation. Still other Quakers believe that the souls of the dead go to either heaven or hell, determined by how one lives while on Earth.

In the Islamic belief, death is not the end of life but rather a time of transition. While on Earth, a Muslim's duty is to prepare for the afterlife by being righteous and practicing the five pillars of Islam: make a declaration of faith; formal prayer; charity; fasting during the month of Ramadan; and making, if able, a pilgrimage to Mecca.

Upon death, Muslims believe angels visit the body in the grave to determine through questioning whether the deceased is a believer or unbeliever. On the Day of Judgment or Resurrection, Islam teaches, there will be a tremendous earthquake that makes mountains crumble. The dead rise up from their graves and are judged. A paradise with bountiful pleasures awaits believers, and a fiery hell is the eternal fate for sinners.

Both Hindus and Buddhists, as well as members of some other Eastern religions, believe that life in the present world is, for the most part, a time of suffering, but people are reincarnated—reborn—again and again in order to be released from a constant cycle known as the law of karma. Under this impersonal law, an individual's deeds—good or bad—determine rewards or punishments in each successive life. In other words, one reaps what one sows.

For Hindus the transition from life to death is not considered frightening, because of the knowledge that rebirth will occur. When Hindus are near death, they attempt to complete any unfinished business, which may include misunderstandings that have not been resolved, obligations that need to be repaid, misdeeds that require apology or forgiveness.

Buddhists also believe in reincarnation and karma and they hope to achieve Nirvana, a state in which a person is liberated from desire—wanting and craving worldly things. In the Buddhist view, after death the spirit of the deceased goes through a process called *bardos*, which includes first recognizing that one has died and then experiencing sensations felt during a lifetime because of one's karma. At the end of the process, a highly developed person who has no more cravings enters Nirvana because there is no reason to be reborn. Reincarnation is required for those who are not yet liberated.

NOTES

1. Ramya Gopal, "How My Faith Honors the Mothers of Tomorrow," *Beliefnet.com*. www.beliefnet.com/story/170/story_17071_1.html (accessed September 14, 2005).
2. Gopal, "How My Faith."
3. Rachel Cushman, "From a Chinook Girl to a Woman," *SNAG*, January 1, 2005. www.snagmagazine.com/index.php?s=23&a=19 (accessed June 9, 2005).
4. Susan Secakuku, *Meet Mindy: A Native Girl from the Southwest* (Washington, D.C.: National Museum of the American Indian, 2003), 14.
5. Quoted in Karen Gravelle, *Soaring Spirits: Conversations with Native American Teens* (Lincoln, NE: iUniverse, 2000), 70.
6. Ami Chen Mills, "MultiCulti Weddings When Catholics, Hindus and Jews Fill the Pews," *Bahá'í News*, June 23, 2002. www.uga.edu/bahai/2002/020623.html (accessed May 22, 2005).
7. PBS, "Dealing with Death," *In the Mix*. www.pbs.org/inthemix/shows/show_death.html (accessed May 23, 2005).
8. Terry Tafoya, quoted in Patricia Anderson, *All of Us: Americans Talk about the Meaning of Death* (New York: Dell, 1996), 155–167.
9. Donia Regis, "God, Why Did You Take My Granny?" *Urban Health Chronicles*, Summer 1999, 3.
10. Quoted in Seon Hye Moon, "What Do You Believe?," *Alternet.org*, June 11, 2002. www.alternet.org/story/13350/ (accessed May 22, 2005).
11. "The Afterlife," *Itsfinished.com*. www.itsfinished.com/teens/someone_afterlife.cfm (accessed September 16, 2005).

7 Lesser-Known Beliefs

> **Being Hindu . . . has directed and guided me to become a better person . . . to be a better student, to gain a better understanding of my own behavior, to always offer service to my friends and to strangers, to show the utmost respect for teachers and parents. . . . It has also taught me that all religions are truth and have to be respected.—Neal A. Chatterjee, *Teen Spirit*[1]**

Bahá'ís. Hare Krishnas. Hindus. Humanists. Jains. Mennonites. Pagans. Pentecostals. Quakers (Society of Friends). Scientologists. Unitarian Universalists. Wiccans. Zoroastrians. How many of these religious groups are familiar to you? Perhaps you've read or heard about some of them, but unless you follow one of these faiths, their central beliefs may be unknown and may even seem mysterious or exotic.

News reporters, book publishers, and television producers frequently contend that large numbers of youth in the United States are turning to faiths outside the mainstream. Not so, according to the National Study of Youth and Religion, conducted from 2001 to 2005 by researchers at the University of North Carolina, Chapel Hill; they surveyed thousands of teens from thirteen to seventeen years old. Researchers found that, contrary to popular opinion, youth in the United States "are not flocking in droves to 'alternative' religions and spiritualities such as paganism and Wicca. Teens who are pagan or Wiccan represent fewer than one-third of 1 percent of U.S.

teens. There are thus twice the number of Jehovah's Witness teens as there are pagan and Wiccan teens." In addition, the researchers concluded, "The vast majority of U.S. teens (like adults) are Christians or not religious. The so-called new immigrant [Eastern] religions are tiny fractions of adolescent religion. Muslim teens represent one-half of 1 percent of U.S. teens, Buddhists less than one-third of 1 percent, and Hindu a mere one-tenth of 1 percent."[2]

While this book can cover only a small number of the religions that are considered outside the mainstream, numerous published and electronic sources explain basic doctrines, rituals, and sacred texts—or lack of them—that guide specific religious and spiritual groups. Following are brief summaries of some lesser-known philosophical and religious beliefs.

BEING A WICCAN; BEING A PAGAN

Wicca has become increasingly popular in the United States, especially among teenage girls. A modern version of witchcraft, Wicca is often labeled a *cult*, but it is in fact recognized by federal court rulings as a legal religion. Wicca is an Earth-based religion that some say dates back to ancient Celtics in the British Isles; others say that it is part of a new religious movement of Pagans or neo-Pagans, which includes more than a million devotees in the United States.[3] In other words, "Wiccans are Pagans, but not all Pagans follow a Wiccan path, in the same way that Baptists are Christians, but not all Christians are Baptists," explain Joyce Higginbotham and River Higginbotham, authors of *Paganism*.[4]

Pagans do not have a set of beliefs but rather one of principles by which they develop personally and spiritually. Those principles are spelled out in *Paganism* and include:

- **Being responsible for the beliefs one adopts, one's actions and spiritual and personal development**
- **Deciding what Deity with whom to form a relationship**
- **Understanding that "each part of the world contains a form of consciousness or spark of intelligence"**

- **Realizing that "each part of the universe can communicate with each other part"**
- **Believing that "consciousness survives after death"[5]**

Pagans and Wiccans believe that there is one higher power, with equal feminine and masculine sides—in other words, goddess and god combined. Followers may practice *majick*, using spells (like prayers) to channel divine energy and bring about positive change. There is no connection to stage magic, tricks performed by magicians; the kind of magic described in *Harry Potter* books or shown in some television shows; or to black magic, linked to Satanism—in fact, Pagans and Wiccans do not believe there is a devil or evil one.

Allison, a seventeen-year-old Wiccan in Indiana who has cast spells explains, "Real magic is more a kind of manifestation of will and the energy toward the goal, like getting a job or giving somebody love." When casting a spell, a Wiccan creates a sacred place, or majick circle, and may visualize angels, spirits, or even comical characters. "I usually call on angels," Allison told a reporter. "You can usually envision a white light of feeling surrounding them. The better visualization you can get, the better the results usually. So you can see like little repairmen working on [the sick person] or something like that. The funnier the better, if it can stick in your mind."[6]

Because Pagans and Wiccans revere nature, they strongly believe in protecting the environment. Many rituals, which are like church services, are conducted in natural settings, and practitioners may worship alone or with a Wiccan group, called a *coven*.

There is no hierarchy in Wicca and no creed. Sarah Macias, who became a Wiccan, noted that she "was born into a Catholic family, baptized and raised that way," but from the time she was eight years old she began to question the teachings of the church and what she perceived as contradictions. At nineteen, she discovered Wicca and was pleased that there was no dogma. "I only had to remember two things: The Wiccan Rede and the Rule of Three. 'An' [if] it harm none, do as ye

Some Wiccans wear jewelry with small Celtic symbols, such as a cross in a circle. Celtic symbols are often seen on monuments like these in Irish and Scottish cemeteries.

will,' and 'Remember that all you do, for good or for bane, returns to you three times.' Definitely spiritual rules I could live by," she explained.[7]

The Rede and Rule of Three are actually the basic ethical instructions for Wiccans. Stated another way, these ethics are "If you do no harm, you may do as you please; if you do harm, it will return to you threefold."

BEING A BAHÁ'Í

"I'm a Bahá'í," states Amy J. in a posting on *Kiwibox.com*, an electronic magazine by and for teens. "What's a Bahá'í? The Bahá'í faith is a religion whose purpose is to unite all the races and peoples in one universal Cause and one common Faith."

Bahá'ís are followers of Bahá'u'lláh, who was preceded by Bab, the founder of the independent religion in Persia (now Iran) in 1844. Followers believe Bahá'u'lláh was God's messenger, who brought the Bahá'í beliefs to the forefront. According to Bahá'ís, along with Bahá'u'lláh there have been many messengers, such as Moses, Jesus Christ, Krishna, Zoroaster, and Muhammad.

For Bahá'ís, earthly existence is preparation for an afterlife, or a spiritual journey that has no ending. Bahá'í believers do not, however, accept the concept of reincarnation or transmigration of the soul. Neither do they believe in a physical heaven or hell. In Amy's words,

> As you may know, the beliefs of almost every religion include the promise of a future when peace and harmony will be established on earth and humankind will live in prosperity. We believe that the promised hour has come and that Bahá'u'lláh is the great Personage whose teachings will enable humanity to build a new world. . . . We believe that there is one God and that mankind is one. We believe in the equality of men and women, we believe in the elimination of prejudices of all kinds. Sound kind of familiar? I think all good people believe these things.[8]

There are no clergy, rituals, rites, or other ceremonies in the Bahá'í religion. Although the center of the faith is in Wilmette, Illinois, where a house of worship is located, followers gather in spiritual assemblies in thousands of communities across the United States. Christene Kruge of New Paltz, New York, learned about the religion at the Wilmette House of Worship. She was seventeen years old at the time and lived in northern Chicago. She went to a Bahá'í picnic, which she described as "so bizarre. There was such a mix of people from different types of backgrounds and they were all interacting and talking. I thought everyone was drunk at first."[9] Kruge then went on to investigate Bahá'í and realized that the religion's beliefs were like her own. She became a Bahá'í by simply proclaiming her belief and receiving a membership card. Her goal, as with others followers, is to develop as a spiritual person.

BEING A "PEACE CHURCH" MEMBER

A relatively small number of Protestant Christian denominations are known as "historic peace churches"—churches with a pacifist tradition. Peace churches include the Amish, Brethren, Mennonites, and Quakers, who separate themselves from the mainline religious groups in the United States. In addition, there are pacifist groups within the Roman Catholic Church, such as Pax Christi.

Pacifists have long been at the forefront of peace movements, have refused to bear arms, even in self-defense, and have opposed war on religious grounds. During wartime, such a stance has prompted discrimination, harassment, and sometimes violence against them.

Hannah S., a Quaker teen who wrote an essay for *Teen Ink*, pointed out that in spite of oppression and hardships because of their peace activism, Quakers have "never attempted to fight fire with fire." Rather they have tried to overcome "hate through their persistent love, caring and compassion." While growing up, Hannah objected to Quakerism and was aware that she and her family were out of the mainstream. She also recalled how classmates taunted, teased, and harassed her for being a Quaker. She was often asked what it meant to be a Quaker and would simply answer "Peace." Yet other belittling questions followed: "'But do Quakers believe in Jesus?' . . . 'Do you churn your own butter?' 'Are you allowed to use electricity?' 'Why aren't you wearing a bonnet?' And always the smart-aleck from the back of the room, arms crossed, smirking, 'Don't you worship the Quaker Oats guy?'"

Eventually in high school Hannah found that Quaker beliefs applied to her own life. As she explained, "I could not attempt to avenge the taunters . . . but instead I passively resisted, and looked inside for strength." As a Quaker, she

> became active in peace marches as the war in Iraq wrought bloodshed, and arranged candlelight vigils for the many sacrificed lives. I discovered my empowering ability to make a difference in the world, and for this I am immensely proud of my Quakerism, my avowed pacifism. Quakerism has taught me the value of love, the power of inner strength, but most importantly, it has taught me that sometimes it isn't the fist or the noisy protests that can really effect change; sometimes just being silent is enough.[10]

CONSCIENTIOUS OBJECTORS

When a nation is at war, those who oppose armed conflict on religious, ethical, or moral grounds may face a formidable crisis, particularly if they are being recruited for the armed forces. During past wars involving the United States, the federal government has enforced selective service laws requiring a draft, or compulsory military service for young men (women are exempt). Many who believed strongly that they could not participate in armed conflict applied for conscientious objector (CO) status, a legal exemption from the armed forces that allows COs to provide alternative services, such as hospital or forestry work.

Thousands of military personnel were granted CO status during World Wars I and II. With the draft reinstated for World War II, a civilian agency called the Selective Service Administration determined who would receive CO status. There were about 3,500 COs during the Korean War. "By the Vietnam War, more than 90 percent of draftees who applied for CO status—more than 171,000—received it," according to attorney J. E. McNeil, the executive director of the Center on Conscience and War. McNeil points out,

> **The end of the Vietnam War brought the end of the draft . . . [and] of course, those seeking CO status were enlisted men and women. Since Vietnam, the military has had the sole job of determining CO status. Today, to obtain such a discharge you must show a change of heart: your belief that you cannot participate in war must have crystallized after you joined. But the right to a CO discharge, unlike CO status during a draft, is not statutory but based on military regulation and thus can be taken away with little fanfare.**
>
> **This is exactly what happened during the 1991 Gulf War, when the Army granted a mere 111 CO discharges. The Army issued an across-the-board stop-loss order prohibiting many discharges and separations. . . . As a result, more than 2,500 military members went to jail rather than participate in the war.[11]**

Today a male U.S. citizen is legally required to register with the Selective Service System within the period from thirty days before his eighteenth birthday to twenty-nine days afterward. The law also applies to many male residents in the United States who are not citizens. Women are not required to register, but they are welcome volunteers in the armed services.

Not all members of churches with a pacifist tradition oppose all wars, and sometimes there are debates within peace churches about when and if government use of military force against a perceived or real enemy is ever justified. Some would say never. Others would argue that violent action may be necessary to bring about justice.

In Calabasas, California, near Los Angeles, the Malibu Hindu temple sits in all its splendor, reflecting just one of the many distinct religious groups and varied traditions in the United States. Photo by Nissa Gay.

BEING A HINDU

Hinduism, some practitioners say, is not a religion; rather, it is a philosophical way of life that originated in India. Hindus from India and other countries total more than one million in the United States.[12]

What does it mean to be a Hindu? The answer can be complex and defies any simple definition because Hinduism is "known to practitioners as Sanatana Dharma, which means everlasting or eternal religion/truth/rule" and is "based on the teachings of ancient sages and scriptures like the Vedas and the Upanishads. The word *dharma* connotes 'that which supports the universe' and effectively means any path of spiritual discipline which leads to God."[13] Yet there are some basic Hindu philosophies that include but are not limited to the following:

- **Hinduism has no human founder, no particular Sabbath day, and no specific dogma.**
- **There is a supreme being called Brahman, but that being is unlike the God of many Western religions. The supreme being—"One that is All"—has no gender and is known by various names because over history in India the different cultures with their varied languages developed their individual concepts of god.**
- **There are millions of gods in Hinduism, and they are seen as divine creations of the supreme being. Stone, metal, or wooden images of deities in homes or temples are symbols of and a**

way to communicate with a supreme being through *puja*, or worship, which involves prayers—usually chants or hymns—and various offerings.

- Ancient scriptures known as the Vedas are the foundation of Hinduism. In Sanskrit, India's oldest written language, Veda means "sacred knowledge."
- Reincarnation is part of Hindu philosophy, which says there is an eternal birth-death-birth cycle, where a soul moves from body to body based on the law of karma. That is, through their actions people create their own destiny. If people live a "good" life, their next life will consist of a higher quality; conversely, "bad" living leads to a lesser quality of life in the next rebirth. A primary goal is to live one's life so that the soul is liberated and a person experiences inner Truth and becomes one with a supreme being.

A Hindu devotee may worship an image of Ganesha (shown here), while another Hindu may worship one or several of the other many Hindu gods, all of whom represent manifestations of a Supreme Being.

- Because of reverence for all life and the belief in *ahimsa*—that one should refrain from harming other beings—many, but certainly not all, Hindus are vegetarians and do not eat meat, fish, fowl, or eggs.
- For Hindus, there is no one path to salvation, and all religions deserve tolerance and understanding.[14]

NOW YOU KNOW!

- Hare Krishnas are part of a communal religious movement officially known as the International Society for Krishna Consciousness. The movement was founded in New York City by A. C. Bhaktivedanta Swami Prabhupada and is based on the philosophy that the Hindu god Krishna is the supreme personal God. Hare Krishnas seek spiritual enlightenment and are known for chanting the mantra "Hare Krishna, Hare Krishna, Krishna Krishna, Hare Hare, Hare Rama, Hare Rama, Rama Rama, Hare Hare."
- Mennonites are Anabaptists and share historical roots with the Amish. But Mennonites differ from the Amish in that they do not separate themselves from society. Historically, they are pacifists, and they believe in simple living, stewardship, and aiding those in need.
- Pentecostals are Protestant Christians, many of whom worship in a highly emotional manner. Some say they become filled with the Holy Spirit and such a sense of joyfulness that they "speak in tongues," garbled utterances called *glossolalia*, which no one has confirmed to be an actual language. In March 2005, Heather Fulcher from Oklahoma City participated in a "Cry Out" conference of 385 teens and leaders calling for revival in their own lives, churches, nation, and world. Fulcher testified, "The Lord came and met with me and He touched me like I've never been touched before. He really released me and told me to stand up and shout my praise to Him and when I did, He really released me and I felt like the burden of the world was lifted off my shoulders."[15]
- Scientologists follow the philosophy of L. Ron Hubbard, who was a successful author of science fiction novels and short stories; he died in 1986. Hubbard proclaimed that a human was a Thetan, neither mind nor body but the essence of a person. He wrote *Dianetics: The Modern Science of Mental Health* and other books to explain his theory about understanding the dynamics that can help a person take control of his or her life. Scientology website declares, "The Scientology religion is about the individual man or woman. Its goal is to bring an individual to a sufficient understanding of himself and his life and free him to make improvements where he finds them necessary and in the ways he sees fit."[16]
- Unitarian Universalists consider themselves members of a liberal religion and do not follow any creed. They "believe that personal experience, conscience and reason should be the final authorities in religion, and that in the end religious authority lies not in a book or person or institution, but in ourselves."[17]
- Zoroastrians follow the teachings of Zoroaster, who was born in Persia (now Iran) and whose writings appear in holy texts called the Avesta. Followers attempt to live by the basic tenets of good thoughts, good words, and good deeds and worship in temples with fire altars. Fire symbolizes God and is thus sacred. As James R. Williams, a Zoroastrian explained, "I am a proud member of an ancient, now small, but vibrant faith. I am a Zoroastrian despite being the only member of my faith at each of the schools I have attended. . . . Mostly I am Zoroastrian because of the inner peace, strength and insights that I regularly gain through the practice of being an active member of my faith."[18]

BEING A JAIN

Jainism originated in India and shares some of the beliefs and cultural roots of Hinduism and Buddhism, such as the belief in karma. In some parts of the United States, Hindus and Jains may worship in the same temples. But Jains consider themselves followers of a separate faith, and estimates on the number of Jains in the United States vary widely, ranging from sixty thousand to one hundred thousand. "Communities exist in most U.S. states and Canadian provinces, but 80 percent of North American Jains live in ten states, dominated by New Jersey (16 percent), California (15 percent), and New York (12 percent), with significant representation in Maryland, Massachusetts, Pennsylvania, Michigan, Ohio, Illinois, and Texas," according to the *New Historical Atlas of Religion in America*.[20]

WHAT IS SANTERIA?

If you have ever watched replays of the 1950s sitcom *I Love Lucy*, no doubt you have seen and heard Cuban entertainer Desi Arnaz, who played Ricky Ricardo, sing Babalú-Ayé while keeping the beat on a drum. But did you know that Ricky Ricardo was honoring a Santeria spirit or god?

The Santeria religion stems from the eighteenth century, when hundreds of thousands of slaves from West Africa were taken to Cuba to labor in the sugar cane fields and mills. When slaves arrived in Cuba, they were forced by Spanish law to follow practices of the Roman Catholic Church and were forbidden to take part in their own religious traditions, which stem from ancient beliefs and rituals of the Yoruba people (a language group) in Africa. However, Yoruba slaves in Cuba found a way to maintain their own religion: they honored their traditional gods while appearing to be devoted to Catholic saints and personages. Church clerics believed that the slaves accepted the Catholic saints as personifications of Yoruba spirits. Thus the religion became known as Santeria, meaning "the way of the saints," and the practice of honoring the Santeria gods spread throughout Cuba.

Santeria came to the United States with Cuban refugees as well as with devotees from the Caribbean, and the practices they brought frequently have been presented as "idolatrous, dangerous, or a product of a backward people," according to Miguel A. De La Torre, who grew up in a Santeria household and is a former believer. But in his book on Santeria, De La Torre disputes these stereotypes and points out the spirituality and rituals that are part of this faith tradition. Although these traditions are not well known by the general public, they are familiar to people in Latin American communities. The religion is widely practiced "in the homes of many Hispanics throughout the United States, especially those of Cuban descent."[19]

The faithful try to pattern their lives after five basic principles: *ahisma* (nonviolence and protection of all life), truthfulness, not being greedy or stealing, monogamy and faithfulness, and nonattachment to material goods. Ahisma is a top priority and includes the belief in peaceful coexistence with animals. As a result many Jains are strict vegetarians and do not eat meat or animal products, limiting their foods to plants. One such practicing Jain is United States–born Jay Shah, an eighteen-year-old medical student at Michigan State University. In his view, "it would be great if everyone could adopt nonviolence, but looking at the world today, I doubt it," Shah told a reporter. "But if you take small steps, you can make a difference."[21]

NOTES

1. Quoted in Paul B. Raushenbush, *Teen Spirit: One World, Many Paths* (Deerfield Beach, FL: Health Communications, 2004), 59.
2. Christian Smith, *Soul Searching: The Religious and Spiritual Lives of American Teenagers*, with Melinda Lundquist Denton (Oxford: Oxford University Press, 2005), 32.
3. Joyce Higginbotham and River Higginbotham, *Paganism: An Introduction to Earth-Centered Religions* (St. Paul, MN: Llewellyn Press, 2004), 1
4. Higginbotham and Higginbotham, *Paganism*, 8.
5. Higginbotham and Higginbotham, *Paganism*, 39–42.
6. Quoted in Jordan Denari and Kelsey Impicciche, "Wiccans Explain Their Religious Beliefs," *Indianapolis Star*, August 22, 2004, J8.
7. Sarah Macias, "Wicca—a Path to Personal Truth," *Ex-Christian.Net*, posted November 20, 2004. www.exchristian.net/testimonies/2004/11/wicca-path-to-personal-truth.php (accessed May 27, 2005).
8. Amy J., "The Bahá'í Faith," *Kiwibox.com*, March 27, 2005. www.kiwibox.com/article.asp?a=33073 (accessed May 28, 2005).
9. Quoted in Rasheed Oluwa, "Young Religion Offers Message of Diversity," *Poughkeepsie Journal* (New York), September 18, 2004, A1.
10. Hannah S., "Quaker Meeting," *Teen Ink*, October 2004. http://teenink.com/Past/2004/October/18170.html (accessed May 30, 2005).

11. J. E. McNeil, "Matters of Conscience," *Legal Times*, August 2, 2004. www.nisbco.org/article/LegalTimesProbono.htm (accessed October 4, 2004).

12. Edwin Scott Gaustan and Philip L. Barlow, *New Historical Atlas of Religion in America* (New York: Oxford University Press, 2000), 272.

13. Subhamoy Das, "An Introduction to Hinduism: How Do You Define Hinduism?" *About.com*. www.hinduism.about.com/library/weekly/extra/bl-intro-define.htm (accessed May 26, 2005).

14. Based on "Hinduism: The Basics," *Hinduism Online*. www.himalayanacademy.com/basics (accessed February 6, 2006), which includes common questions—and answers—about Hinduism, karma and reincarnation, Hinduism gods, and a lexicon of important terms in Hinduism.

15. Heather Fulcher, TWIN Cry Out Conference, March 14–15, 2005, Falcon, North Carolina.

16. See Church of Scientology, "Scientology Success: Family, Marriage, Relationships." www.scientology.org/html/en_US/results/index.html (accessed February 6, 2006).

17. See Unitarian Universalist Association, "About Unitarian Universalism." www.uua.org/aboutuu/ (accessed February 6, 2006).

18. Quoted in Raushenbush, *Teen Spirit*, 64–65.

19. Miguel A. De La Torre, *Santeria: The Beliefs and Rituals of a Growing Religion in America* (Grand Rapids, MI: William B. Eerdmans, 2004), xii, xvii.

20. Edwin Scott Gaustan and Philip L. Barlow, *New Historical Atlas of Religion in America* (New York: Oxford University Press, 2000), 272.

21. Quoted in Niraj Warikoo, "The Jainism Way of Life: Religion of Nonviolence Marks 30 Years Locally," *Detroit Free Press*, May 16, 2005. www.freep.com.

8 What Agnostics and Atheists Believe

> **I consider myself an atheist because . . . I don't believe there is a higher power that controls everything. I believe that the universe is chaotic and random, and that there's not a lot of sense to it.**
> **—Susan Allen, high school senior[1]**

An agnostic teen writing for Kiwibox.com explains that she believes "there is something out there" but that she doesn't believe it's god." She acknowledges, "I still ask questions about different religions everyday," but she is convinced that "there's just so much that people do not understand about religion and nobody will ever fully understand it."[2]

Though many agnostics may have a more complicated explanation about their beliefs, the idea that "there is something out there" and it may or may not be God is a simple summary of what agnosticism is. A more detailed definition is posted on the *Atheism Web*:

> An agnostic is someone who believes that we do not know for sure whether God exists. Some agnostics believe that we can never know. In recent years, however, the term agnostic has also been used to describe those who simply believe that the evidence for or against God is inconclusive, and therefore are undecided about the issue.[3]

CHECK IT OUT!

The hero of *Godless*, an award-winning teen novel by Pete Hautman, is Jason Bock, who rebels against his parents' religious beliefs and asks many serious questions about the existence of a god. But the story, told from Jason's point of view, is full of wry humor and vivid imagination as this sixteen-year-old relates his experiences and those of his three friends who join him in a quest to establish their own god—their town's water tower. Jason calls his invented god the Ten-Legged One and names the disciples Chutengodians.

Jason's friend Shin begins to write a bible for the new religion, with portions heading each chapter, such as "And the sun rose and the sun set and the waters of the Earth did moisten that which was dry, and the Humans did drink thirstily of it, and the Chutengodians did worship the Ten-Legged One and all of the Ocean's Avatars, and lo, there were times of goodness and plenty."[4]

As the story progresses, the Chutengodians climb the water tower for a ceremony, and from then on one dangerous situation after another arises. Jason finds himself in trouble with his and his friends' parents and the police. While he regrets endangering the followers of his fake religion and envies those who have a sincere belief, he still remains an agnostic, if not an outright atheist.

Atheists have a more explicit view, such as the perspective that was presented by a *St. Petersburg Times* columnist who wrote,

> Though I was brought up in a religious faith, it was at a very young age—preteen—that I realized I had no belief in God and no amount of indoctrination was going to change that. . . . Just to be clear, it is not just God that I can't fathom. I also reject the existence of Satan or any form of afterlife beyond the redistribution of the body's matter. . . . My view is that the "soul" does not exist outside a functioning brain, nothing was "meant to be," and things that seem inexplicable are not miracles or paranormal experiences, they are simply not yet explained. I have never understood why the fallback position to unanswerable questions about the universe is that an all-powerful, all-knowing being intervened. To me, "we don't know yet" is a fine response.[5]

In the National Survey of Youth and Religion, researchers found that 1.4 percent of all U.S. teens "consider themselves atheists. The same number consider themselves agnostics. This is roughly the same proportion of American adults (about 2 percent) who identify explicitly as atheist or agnostic."[6]

HARASSING NONRELIGIOUS STUDENTS

In a nation that prides itself on the right of individuals to believe whatever they choose, there have been numerous instances of harassment of people who profess to be atheists or agnostics. Students who "come out" and say that they are agnostics or atheists and live in conservative communities report that Christian classmates, teachers, ministers, youth leaders, and others all too often want to "save" them. It's a common complaint in letters posted on "Smart Kids," a page on the American Atheists' website.

One teen reported that when his classmates became aware that he was an atheist, he became "every christian's private conversion project." Another wrote, "Everyone knows I am an Atheist, but they still seemed convinced that they can convert me." They asked questions such as "Why don't you come to my youth group?" "You could go to my church camp this summer," "Why don't you just come with me to church?" "Will we see you at the pole?" (The "pole" refers to the flagpole on school grounds where some students gather before classes to pray, a common practice in some schools across the United States.)

Jeanette, a sixteen-year-old, wrote, "My being an atheist has led to all sorts of negative consequences: I don't get parts in the musicals directed by a fundamentalist teacher, I am looked at as a possible security hazard (because atheists, apparently, are ALWAYS school shooters) and I am scorned by students." Nevertheless, Jeanette saw a positive side to her experiences: "Maybe I'm not in the musical, but I can think for myself. I am a rational, individualistic person, and my thoughts don't rely upon the thoughts of others. I do not obey blindly."[7]

Dan reported that when he was in middle school, he was tormented "on a daily basis because of my atheism." He told about a classmate he was forced to sit by at lunch:

> As soon as I sit down, the first thing I hear is "Still not gonna face the truth, eh?" I respond "I'm not in the mood today,

> Andy, maybe we can discuss this some other time" then I tried to change the subject . . . but his mind was fixed like a laser on conversion, and he wouldn't let up. We proceeded into a fairly civilized argument, in which I shot down all of his arguments and threw some at him. Seeing that he clearly was completely defeated, he resorted to the classic "only god knows" line. . . . Later that day, in US History, our teacher left the room and everyone started talking. Our names are alphabetically ordered so I had to sit next to [Andy]. "How do you feel, Dan," he said with an annoying tone. "About what?" I replied. "About knowing that you're gonna burn in hell . . . "[8]

Dan told Andy to "shut up," although he felt bad about it afterward because he and Andy had once been friends. Dan finally went to a counselor to get his seat assignment changed and noted that he has no regrets about ending his relationship with Andy.

To protect themselves from verbal attacks and sometimes outright physical harm, some young atheists do not reveal to others what they believe. Teens say that they have also learned that it's not necessarily helpful to argue with the pious and with those who believe they have *the* answers regarding religion. "Whenever someone asks me if I believe in god, I simply turn around and ask them 'Why do you believe in god?'" one teen wrote. "It is amazing how many people can think of no response other than 'because I was brought up to' or 'because the bible says so.' . . . It is amazing how asking someone to question their faith really makes them realize they have no reason for worshipping as they do."[9]

DISCRIMINATING AGAINST ATHEISTS

An eighteen-year-old atheist, Dina Dukhanova, who is also an immigrant, wrote an article for the *Salem Headlight*, noting,

> I'm a member of a minority that is routinely disregarded and discriminated against in America. I hold a belief based on which more Americans would refuse to vote for me if I were running for office than based on any other belief or

> characteristic. When I talk about this discrimination, I am . . . constantly laughed at and told that it's not real discrimination and I have no basis for complaining.[10]

Regardless of the common view that atheists don't experience "real discrimination," the facts indicate otherwise. As Dukhanova stated, most U.S. politicians would not admit to being an atheist or agnostic and run for election expecting to win. Such a politician would immediately be labeled with any number of derogatory terms. In addition, at least seven state constitutions forbid people to hold office if they happen to be atheists or agnostics. The Texas constitution, for one, says that a person can be "excluded from holding office" if she or he doesn't "acknowledge the existence of a Supreme Being." Such language would also bar most Buddhists and some Unitarians and New Age religionists who do not believe in a personal deity.[11] State constitutions that carry similar language include North Carolina's, which states, "No person shall be eligible to the office of Governor who denies the existence of the Supreme Being," and Tennessee's, which says, "No person who denies the being of God, or a future state of rewards and punishments, shall hold any office in the civil department of this state."

In spite of such language, these bans have not been enforced. The laws violate the U.S. Constitution, which states that "no religious Test shall ever be required as a Qualification to any Office or public Trust under the United States."[12]

Proof of discrimination is very real for someone like Richard Sherman, who in 2005 applied for a teaching position at a high school in a Chicago suburb. Richard is the son of Robert I. Sherman, a prominent atheist and activist. Throughout his life, the younger Sherman has often been associated with his father's actions, such as protests against the Pledge of Allegiance in public school. Yet Richard was not asked about his political or religious beliefs when he was interviewed in February and April 2005 for a teaching position. According to *Chicago Tribune* columnist Eric Zorn, Sherman was offered a job in the science department of the Schaumburg High School, received welcoming e-mails, and "had an orientation meeting with [the] district personnel director Robert Grimm in which he signed various papers and received information on employment benefits." But a few days later, Grimm asked Sherman to meet with him because the district had "serious concerns" about him. Grimm told Sherman that his "philosophies on teaching didn't mesh well with those of other teachers and division heads" at the school. Thus, Grimm would not recommend that the school board hire Sherman. As columnist Zorn wrote, "Such an abrupt and peculiar withdrawal of a job offer would raise significant questions under any circumstances. But here it raises an odor as well—the smell of fear, of religious intolerance and injustice."

The young Sherman is his own man with his own religious beliefs and his own agenda—teaching, not crusading. If the fact that his father is one of the most controversial public figures in the northwest suburbs played any role in the sudden withdrawal of the job offer, it would, as he put it, amount to a blatant "moral and ethical breach."[13]

Discrimination against atheists in the workplace is a common topic when atheists gather and share experiences about losing jobs and being shunned by coworkers and neighbors because of their beliefs. No one knows how often atheists experience discrimination, but Margaret Downey, president of the Freethought Society of Greater Philadelphia, has been keeping a database of incidents since 1999. The Freethought Society is a member group of the national Atheist Alliance, which, along with American Atheists, met in an annual convention held in Philadelphia in spring 2005. According to a news report, Downey has recorded more than two hundred

Now You Know!

In 1987 Robert I. Sherman was a reporter for an atheist magazine, and he interviewed then–presidential candidate George H. W. Bush. When Sherman asked Bush whether he recognized the equal citizenship and patriotism of American atheists, Bush replied, "I don't know that atheists should be considered as citizens, nor should they be considered patriots. This is one nation under God."

cases of "discrimination events . . . ranging from the seemingly petty to the evidently serious." These include

> a woman in Greenville, Tennessee, who was fired after coworkers discovered that she was an atheist; a principal in Madison, Wisconsin, who collected the names of students who declined to recite the Pledge of Allegiance; and an eleven-year-old girl in Abilene, Texas, who was told by a substitute teacher that she had "no right to live in America because she refused to say the 'under God' [in the] Pledge of Allegiance."[14]

SCOUT'S HONOR?

For the past two decades, the Boy Scouts of America (BSA) has been under fire for excluding atheists and homosexuals from membership, despite the fact that the organization has a congressional charter mandating them to be "open to all boys." A highly publicized case occurred in 2002 when nineteen-year-old Darrell Lambert of Washington state was kicked out of the Scouts because he is an avowed atheist. A member of the Scouts for more than ten years, Lambert had won several dozen merit badges and achieved the highest ranking as an Eagle Scout and hoped to be a Scout leader. But while at a training conference, he told others about his beliefs and declared that he thought it was wrong to bar kids who don't believe in a god.

The organization's leaders quickly reacted, saying Lambert had to choose between his beliefs or a belief in a supreme being and loyalty to the Scout's Oath, which states, "On my honor I will do my best to do my duty to God and my country and to obey the Scout Law; To help other people at all times; To keep myself physically strong, mentally awake, and morally straight."

Lambert was given ten days to make his choice, but he could not profess to believing in a supreme being. As a result he was soon informed that he was no longer welcome in the Scouts. Although Lambert has appealed his expulsion to regional and national Scout officials, the Scouts maintain that they have the right as a private organization to exclude not only atheists but also homosexuals from membership. Indeed, this membership criterion was upheld in 2000 by the U.S. Supreme Court, which ruled that BSA was exempt from antidiscrimination laws.

To reinforce its exclusionary measure, the Executive Board of the BSA issued a resolution the following year that states in part:

> The national officers agree with [a task force] report that "duty to God is not a mere ideal for those choosing to associate with the Boy Scouts of America; it is an obligation," which has defined good character for youth of Scouting age throughout Scouting's 92–year history and that the Boy Scouts of America has made a commitment "to provide faith-based values to its constituency in a respectful manner;" . . .
>
> The national officers further agree that homosexual conduct is inconsistent with the traditional values espoused in the Scout Oath and Law and that an avowed homosexual cannot serve as a role model for the values of the Oath and Law."[15]

Lambert hopes to continue his fight to convince BSA that the organization should be inclusive, and he has the support of such national groups as Scouting for All; Inclusive Scouting.net, the Secular Coalition of America, humanists, and atheists. But it is an uphill fight. As humanists point out, "Scouting has a long and well-documented history of exclusion involving non-theistic belief systems such as Humanism, atheism, Buddhism, and Unitarian Universalism."[16]

Nevertheless, protests against BSA have been ongoing. Because of BSA's discriminatory policies, dozens of United Way chapters across the United States have cut off funding to BSA organizations; in some states, Scouts have been evicted from tax-supported parks and campsites.

One individual protest came from *Washington Post* staff writer Rick Weiss, who wrote that he had probably investigated more religions than most people but is an atheist. After reading about Lambert's ouster from BSA, he wrote a column decrying the BSA position and asking, "What if I gave up my atheism to serve a God who demands I toss a virgin into a volcano once a year? What if I chose to align myself with a God who demands

What's Your Opinion?

It's common for many high school, college, and professional sports teams in the United States to have a prayer before a game. Usually, the prayer is led by a Christian minister or chaplain, since Christianity is the dominant religion. But what if someone on a sports team is an agnostic or atheist? Because an atheist doesn't believe in God, what should athletes who are nonreligious do? Should they be "team players" no matter what and go against their beliefs? And if teammates insist that their performance or game win is due to their prayers, what should a nonbeliever's response be?

At many public events, whether in schools or public places, people may be asked to stand for a moment of silence in place of listening to someone lead a prayer. Should an atheist be required to join in? If atheists stand up, is this a sign that they now accept the religious belief that prayer is a way to petition a deity? If atheist students must respect the religious and stand in silent prayer, should the religious show their respect for atheists? If so, how?

that I kill all infidels? Would I be a better Scout for believing in a God who says all those who believe in other Gods are destined for hell? Is that what Scouting is about?" Weiss reported that he dug out his old Eagle badge and returned it to Scout headquarters with a note saying he "had not realized what a small God I had aligned myself with when I took the Boy Scout Oath."[17]

NOTES

1. Quoted in Aidan Seale-Feldman, "I Am an Atheist," *Paly Voice*, April 30, 2005. http://voice.paly.net/view_story.php?id=2551 (accessed February 6, 2006); originally appeared in *Verde Magazine*, February 14, 2005.

2. stonertweak420, "Agnostic," *Kiwibox.com*, April 19, 2005. www.kiwibox.com/article.asp?a=33085 (accessed June 3, 2005).

3. Mathew, "An Introduction to Atheism," *Atheism Web*. www.infidels.org/news/atheism/intro.html (accessed June 6, 2005).

4. Pete Hautman, *Godless* (New York: Simon & Schuster, 2004), 111.

5. Robyn E. Blumner, "I'm an Atheist—So What?" *St. Petersburg Times*, August 8, 2004, p. 6P.

6. Christian Smith, *Soul Searching: The Religious and Spiritual Lives of American Teenagers*, with Melinda Lundquist Denton (Oxford: Oxford University Press, 2005), 86.

7. Quoted in American Atheists, "Smart Kids." www.atheists.org/family/html/body_smart_kids.html (accessed June 5, 2005).

8. American Atheists, "Smart Kids."

9. American Atheists, "Smart Kids."

10. Dina Dukhanova, "Freedom of Religion Means Freedom from Religion, Too," *Salem Headlight*, April 11, 2002, posted on an Internet forum, April 25, 2002. http://listproc.ucdavis.edu/archives/thesoapbox/log0204/0015.html (June 6, 2005).

11. "Religious Discrimination in U.S. State Constitutions," *ReligiousTolerance.org*, October 19, 2000. www.religioustolerance.org/texas.htm (accessed June 6, 2005).

12. See August Berkshire, "State Discrimination against Atheists," *Minnesota Atheists*. www.mnatheists.org/stateconst.html (accessed June 6, 2005).

13. Eric Zorn, "Atheists Son Deserves Job on His Own Merits," *Chicago Tribune*, May 26, 2005. www.chicagotribune.com.

14. Doron Taussig, "Losing Your Religion," *Citypaper.net*, March 24–30, 2005. http://citypaper.net/articles/2005-03-24/cb.shtml (accessed June 6, 2005).

15. Boy Scouts of America, "Resolution," February 6, 2002. www.scouting.org/media/press/020206/resolution.html (accessed June 17, 2005).

16. Mary Ellen Sikes, "American Boy Scout Expelled for Nonbelief," Institute for Humanist Studies, August 11, 2004. www.iheu.org/modules/wfsection/article.php?articleid=474 (June 17, 2005).

17. Rick Weiss, "For Me, It Was Never about God," *Washington Post*, November 17, 2002, B1.

9 Getting to Know Others' Beliefs

Among all U.S. age groups, teens are the most likely to express interest in and want to know about religious practices and traditions not related to their own or their family's beliefs.[2]

> **I believe labels like Hindu, Christian, and whatever separates humanity. If we just all realize that most of us are on the same search; the search for God and truths, the world would be a better place.—Teen known as SeekerOfTruth on *Beliefnet.com*[1]**

Visiting a place of worship other than your own and spending time with a person whose faith is not the same as yours can set the stage for learning about the great diversity of American religious traditions. Sometimes it is a matter of being open to classmates of varied faiths, races, and national backgrounds. Seventeen-year-old Swetha Rao Surapaneni of California put it this way:

> When I started elementary school, all my friends were Indian Hindu. We got along well together because we shared the same values and beliefs. Then I got to know other "Asians," including kids who were Chinese, Japanese, Korean, and Taiwanese. I discovered that I was similar to these people in many ways. In high school, my group of friends expanded even more to include kids who are Caucasian, Mexican, and African American. I even know some Christian Indians. For me, all of these different influences have helped me a lot. Our Hindu religion tells us not

> to put down others, or to try and convert them, but rather to try and learn from them and embrace them.[3]

Another way to meet people of other faiths is to get involved in an interfaith youth project, which is usually a service project that brings together religiously diverse people. Habitat for Humanity is one example. Habitat participants come from varied economic and social backgrounds, races, and religions and work with needy families to build houses. Among other service projects that are likely to include people with diverse religious beliefs are programs to feed the hungry, house the homeless, and aid senior citizens. Additional projects include antihate, antidiscrimination, and peace efforts.

INTERFAITH COUNCILS AND EVENTS

Numerous cities and towns across the United States have established interfaith councils that frequently sponsor speakers for activities and events that foster appreciation for diverse religious beliefs. An interfaith council in Minnesota, for instance, helped find speakers for a 2005 event called "Learning about the Faiths of Our Neighbors," which was planned by the Lester Park United Methodist Church in Lakeville. "Part of loving our neighbors is understanding and respecting who they are and what they believe," noted the church's minister, the Reverend David Werner. The summer-long event included a weekly barbecue and, afterward, a speaker and question-and-answer session. According to a news report, speakers in the series were from such faith traditions as "Roman Catholicism, Judaism, Unitarian Universalism, Bahaism, Christian Science, Islam, Mormonism, Greek Orthodoxy, Jehovah's Witness, Messianic Judaism, Hinduism, Buddhism, Quakerism and Sufism." Werner pointed out, "through the process of research, we found faith traditions we didn't even know were in the community."[4]

On many high school and university campuses, students can get involved with a variety of interfaith outreach programs or activities. Consider a "Religion on Campus" event in 2004 at the University of Southern California, Los Angeles. It began with a service described as

> a whirlwind tour of world religions. One minute the gospel choir Saved by Grace is rocking [a conference center] with "Glory to God." The next, a young woman who identifies herself as "a pagan and a Wiccan" is calling on the four elements to "bless this space." A Quaker student leads the assembly in silent worship, then starts a "hand chain." Ankle bells and bangles churning, a silk-garbed dancer interprets the nine emotions of humanity as invocation to Brahma. A Jewish student chants the *Hashkiveinu*, calling down God's shelter of peace. In dramatic monologue, a Christian leader conjures an eye-witness account of how Jesus turned water into wine. A young man faces east and intones the *Adhan,* or Muslim call to prayer. A Buddhist monk pounds ecstatically on the Dharma drum.[5]

Another type of opportunity to get involved is a National Day of Interfaith Youth Service (NDIYS), an annual event that has brought together religiously diverse youth in communities across the nation. The Interfaith Youth Core, based in Chicago, coordinates NDIYS. Founded in 1998, the Interfaith Youth Core is a group of religiously diverse youth who have a common interest in integrating faith, diversity, and social action. According to its mission statement, the organization "seeks to build a movement that encourages religious young people to strengthen their religious identity, foster inter-religious understanding and cooperate to serve the common good."[6]

A popular T-shirt or sweatshirt for sale on several websites and in some stores carries a religious unity symbol, CoeXisT, representing the three monotheistic religions: C is in the shape of the Islamic crescent moon; X is in the shape of the Jewish Star of David; and T is shaped like the Christian cross.

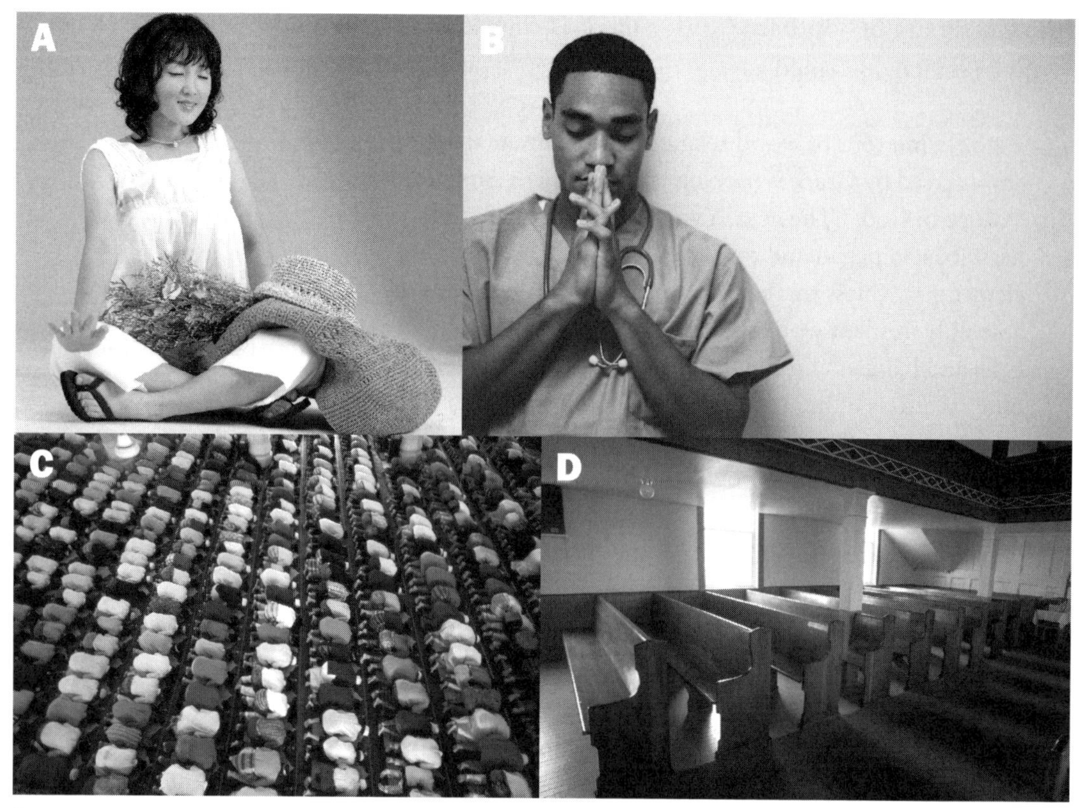

People seek spiritual or divine guidance in a variety of places and diverse ways. In the examples shown here, *A*, a young woman meditates; *B*, a medical professional takes a prayerful stance; *C*, Muslims attend a prayer service in an Islamic mosque; and, *D*, church pews await a religious congregation.

During a NDIYS, youth serve their communities and also share their beliefs, although they are not allowed to proselytize; they work toward better understanding of each other's faiths. One teen who took part said that the day "made me think critically about my own faith and the ways I put that faith into action." Another commented, "I really learned a lot about other religions and in doing so I discovered more about my own religion and myself in general."[7]

After working on projects together, some youth have established interfaith alliances, dialogue groups, or other ongoing efforts to share religious beliefs. Michael, a Jewish teen and founding member of Muslim and Jewish Youth of Chicago, noted that "one of the greatest dangers in this post–11th-of-

September world" is "writing off one color or culture as inhuman." For him it is important to remove barriers through dialogue, which "leads to the recognition of the human."[8]

NDIYS has provided a toolkit for leaders who want to organize an interfaith service day, and it is available on the Internet.[9] The toolkit includes information on how to organize a steering committee, develop a timetable, select appropriate service projects, raise funds, get publicity, and conduct activities that help foster interfaith dialogue. One of those activities involves creating an interfaith map of one's home community or region and marking religious and sacred sites, including places of worship, memorials, and other locations that have religious or spiritual significance, such as burial grounds and ceremonial sites considered sacred to indigenous people.

CHECK IT OUT!

A number of books provide helpful information that can lead to some basic understandings of a variety of religious practices. Some examples are *The Complete Idiot's Guide to World Religions*, by Brandon Toropov and Father Luke Buckles; *The Everything World's Religions Book*, by Robert Pollock; and *I Believe In . . .*, by Pearl Gaskins.

The book *Teen Spirit: One World, Many Paths*, by Paul B. Raushenbush, poses questions about religion that many teens ask, and the author, a *Beliefnet.com* columnist and pastor, answers them in a succinct manner. In addition, within the book, thirteen people explain why they follow a particular religion: Unitarian Universalist, Orthodox Christian, Jewish, Wiccan, Hindu, Zoroastrian, Christian (Protestant/Evangelical), Roman Catholic, Sikh, Bahá'í, Muslim, Mormon, Buddhist.

Some websites also provide information about diverse religious and spiritual traditions. Examples are those of Beliefnet (www.beliefnet.com), the Pluralism Project (www.pluralism.org), Religious Tolerance (www.religioustolerance.org), Interfaith Youth Core (www.ifyc.org), and Spirituality in Higher Education (www.spirituality.ucla.edu).

Interfaith weekend retreats are other avenues for learning about religions other than one's own. For example, youth groups who attend may present short programs telling about their faith or perform a play or rap music describing their religion. At one retreat teens created a canvas mural depicting diverse religious symbols. The completed mural was framed and displayed at each of the faith groups represented.

HEALING POLES

In a demonstration of Native spirituality and outreach to all faiths, master carver Jewell Praying Wolf James of the Lummi tribe in Washington state volunteered in 2002 to carve a healing pole as a memorial to those killed in the 2001 terrorist attack in New York City. The cedar-log carving includes an eagle, "the sacred symbol of Native American spirituality. It is also the symbol chosen to be representative of the original States that joined the Union," James explained. Thirteen arrows in the eagle's claws signify "the lessons learned by the 13 Colonies from the Iroquois Confederacy: strength through unity." In addition, "the Bald Eagle is the figure that represents the sky power (Father Sky) of the Mother Earth religion of Native America." As a male figure, it also symbolizes the fathers that died in the attack on the World Trade Center. A bear mother carved into the pole is a Mother Earth symbol to remember mothers killed by terrorists, and a bear child "represents the nurturing vision of healing through hope and the gifts of life, liberty, and the pursuit of happiness."

The pole was painted with the traditional colors used in Pacific Northwest totem art: red, black, white, and yellow. In James's words, "the four colors represent the 'four races' of humanity that were victimized in the attack upon the World Trade Center."[10] When completed, the healing pole traveled on a flat-bed trailer across the United States and in September 2002 reached Arrow Park in Sterling Forest, one hour north of Manhattan. There, the Lummi say, the Healing Pole "carries a message of hope for harmony and healing in all our relations that comes from America's First Peoples."[11]

The following year Lummi carvers completed a second totem, called the Honoring Pole, which made the cross-country journey to Shanksville, Pennsylvania, where terrorists attacked. As it traveled forty-three hundred miles, the Lummi expedition stopped for sacred ceremonies at various reservations along the West Coast, across Nevada, Arizona, and Colorado, and into the Northeast.

In 2004, two more poles, named Liberty and Freedom, linked by a cross bar, were placed at the Pentagon, where a third terrorist attack occurred. After a few days, Liberty and Freedom were moved to the Historic Congressional Cemetery and stood there for a year. The permanent home for these poles is in the Pentagon Memorial Grove, on Kingman Island.

Narratives about the poles have been posted on the Internet, and one points out that "the most important message" of the carvings is

> that we, the Native People, have not forgotten. We have not forgotten the importance of service and sacrifice. We have not forgotten the importance of healing that which grieves us, as a Nation. We have not forgotten that we are all related, all come from one Creator, and that only good can come when with respect and humility we focus on the forces that bring us together.[12]

The idea of focusing on "forces that bring us together" is no doubt shared by countless spiritual and religious people, as well as those who are nonreligious. Ricardo Melendez of Native American Chumash heritage puts it this way, "Everything we are is part of everything around us—part of a whole system and if we do something to that system we do it to ourselves."[13]

Melendez is community outreach coordinator of Wishtoya (meaning "bridge"), a Chumash foundation in southern California. The foundation endeavors to bridge cultures to enhance understanding about the spiritual relationship between nature and humans.

Attempting to understand, accept, and respect another's beliefs can be a lifelong pursuit, which sometimes begins with

Ricardo Melendez of Mexican and Chumash heritage lives in Southern California. A tribal legend says that thousands of years ago his ancient Chumash ancestors crossed from Santa Cruz Island, off the shore of California, to the mainland via a rainbow bridge, or *wishtoyo*. Photo by Nissa Gay.

book learning. But a member of an interfaith youth leadership council in Houston, Texas, noted, "I've learned that book knowledge about a particular faith doesn't compare to having real relationships with someone from another faith."[14] And perhaps such relationships, if they occur nationwide, can lead to increased interfaith cooperation and high regard for the many diverse religious traditions and spiritual beliefs in America.

NOTES

1. Posted at What Religion? *BeliefNet.com*, December 7, 2002. www.beliefnet.com/boards/message_list.asp?pageID=4&discussionID=182420&messages_per_page=4 (accessed October 20, 2004).

2. D. Michael Lindsay, "Youth on the Edge: A Profile of American Teens (Results of a Gallup Youth Survey)," *Christian Century*, October 4, 2003, 26+.

3. "Finding Self Identity," *Hinduism Today*, October–December 2004. www.hinduismtoday.com/archives/2004/10-12/58_teens.shtml (accessed September 14, 2005).

4. Quoted in Sarah Fleener, "Lester Park Church Spends Summer Learning about Other Faiths," *Duluth Budgeteer News*, June 10, 2005. www.duluth.com/placed/index.php?sect_rank=1&story_id=202879.

5. Diane Krieger, "Leap of Faiths," *USC Trojan Family Magazine*, Summer 2004, 34.

6. See Interfaith Youth Core, "Mission." www.ifyc.org/mission.php (accessed June 18, 2005).

7. Quoted on Interfaith Youth Core, "National Days of Interfaith Youth Service." www.ifyc.org/ndiys/index.html (accessed June 25, 2005).

8. "Muslim and Jewish Teens Build Understanding through Dialogue and Action," *Shma*, May 2005. www.shma.com/may05/ifyc.htm (accessed June 23, 2005).

9. See Interfaith Youth Core. http://ifyc.org/pdf/ndiys_quickstart.pdf.

10. Jewell James, "Lummi Healing Pole." www.lummihealingpole.org/1/story.htm (accessed June 25, 2005).

11. Lummi Healing Pole, "The Lummi Healing Pole Story." www.lummihealingpole.org/1/index.htm (accessed June 25, 2005).

12. Lummi Healing Pole, "Narrative of the 2003 Honoring Pole," September 2003. www.lummihealingpole.org/2/index.htm (accessed June 25, 2005).

13. Ricardo Melendez, taped remarks, December 2004.

14. Quoted in Paul B. Raushenbush, *Teen Spirit: One World, Many Paths* (Deerfield Beach, FL: Health Communications, 2004), 182.

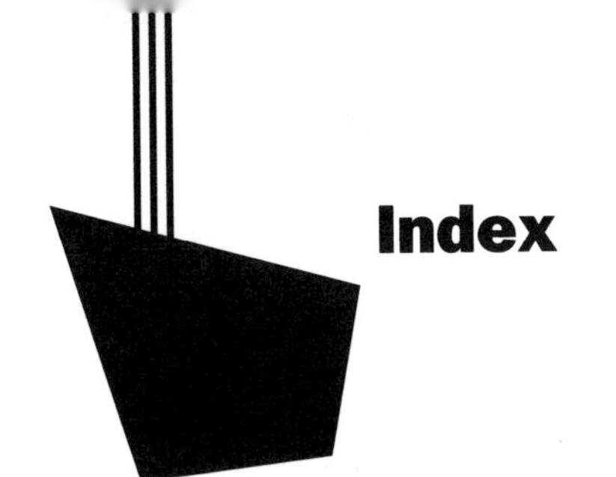

Index

abortion, 38, 44–47, 50
adoption, 44
agnostics, 3, 5, 28, 69, 109–11, 113, 117
American Civil Liberties Union (ACLU), 21, 23, 30
American Indian Religious Freedom Act, 60–61
Amish, 8–9, 58–59, 85–86, 100, 104
Anabaptists, 59
Arab Americans, 10
atheists, 5, 28, 57, 69, 109–17

Bahá'ís, 5, 69, 95, 98–99, 122, 125
Baptists, 8, 11–12, 18, 40, 96
bar mitzvah, 85
bat mitzvah, 85
Bible clubs, 26–29
big bang theory, 30–31
Bill of Rights, 17–18
boy scouts, 115
Bruderhof community, 71
Buddha in Your Backpack: Everyday Buddhism for Teens, 70
Buddhists, 32, 45, 62, 70, 89, 91, 93–94, 96, 113, 123, 125
Bush, President George W., 43, 47, 50

Catholics, 5, 7–8, 11, 25–26, 30
Christian Science, 122
Christianity, 3, 6–8, 37–38, 58, 117
Christians, 4, 6, 17, 27, 29, 37–39, 45, 59–60, 65, 72–74, 82, 85–88, 91–92, 96, 104, 111, 117, 121, 125; Coalition, 22; cross, 20–21, 123; definition, 7; denominations, 13, 17, 38, 92, 99; diversity among, 5–8; faith, 62, 67; groups, 8, 24, 41; nation, 21; values, 39. *See also* Baptists; Catholics; Christian Science; Greek Orthodox; Jehovah's Witnesses; Mennonites; Mormons; Pentecostals; Protestants; Quakers; Seventh-Day Adventists
Church of Jesus Christ of Latter Day Saints. *See* Mormons
circumcision, 81
Civil Rights Act of 1964, 63
The Complete Idiot's Guide to World Religions, 125

conscientious objectors, 101
conservatives, 38–39, 41, 48, 58, 65, 111
creation science, 29, 31
creationism, 29–31
Creator, 32, 60, 65, 127

Decalogue, 21–24
Doe v. Santa Fe Independent School District, 26

Employment Division, Department of Human Resources of Oregon, et al. v. Smith, et al., 60
Equal Access Act, 27–28
establishment clause, 18, 24, 31–32
Everson v. Board of Education, 18
The Everything World's Religions Book, 125
evolution, 29–31

faith healing, 56
First Amendment, 18, 32
Five Pillars of Islam, 11, 21–22, 93
Fraternal Order of Eagles, 23

Genesis, 29–30, 81
Godless, 110
Greek Orthodox, 8, 12–13, 74–75, 82, 87, 92, 122

Hare Krishnas, 95, 104
heaven, 5, 54, 66, 82; and hell, 91–93, 99
Hindus, 5, 45, 69–70, 87, 89, 91, 93, 95–96, 102–5, 121–22, 125; bindi, 2; coming-of-age ceremony, 81–83; creation stories, 32; festival of lights, 62; student council, 73
Hispanics, 67–68, 105
holiday exhibits, 24–25
holy days, 62, 73
homosexuality, 39–43
Humanist, 24, 95, 116

"In God We Trust," 1
in vitro fertilization, 44, 46–47
indigenous people, 4, 32, 125
intelligent dcsign, 29–30
Islam. *See* Five Pillars of Islam; Muslims

Jains, 95, 105–6
Jefferson, Thomas, 18–19
Jehovah's Witnesses, 8, 55–56, 69, 96, 122
Jesus, 7–8, 13, 20, 24, 38, 53, 67, 73–74, 92, 99–100, 123
Jews, 8–9, 25, 73–74, 90–92
Judaism, 3, 5, 8–9, 45, 67, 73, 81, 85, 122

Katelyn's Affection, 68
King, Reverend Martin Luther, Jr., 38

Lee v. Weisman, 26
liberal, 38

McCreary County v. American Civil Liberties Union, 23
Mecca, 11, 91, 93
Mennonites, 68
miracle, 1, 67–68
Moore, Roy, 22
Mormons, 8, 11, 25–26, 45, 53–54, 66, 69, 122, 125

Muslims, 5, 10–12, 62, 68, 73, 81, 89, 91, 93, 96, 123–25

National Day of Interfaith Youth Service (NDIYS), 123–25
National Study of Youth and Religion, 65, 95
Native Americans, 3–5, 32, 58, 60, 75–78, 81, 83–85, 89, 126–27
nativity scene, 24–25

Pagan, 3, 5, 24, 68, 88, 95–97, 123
Pentecostals, 55, 95, 104
peyote, 60–61
Pledge of Allegiance, 56–58, 113, 115
polygamy, 53–54
Protestants, 5, 7, 24, 99, 104, 125; church, 59–60; denominations, 11, 82, 92, 99; evangelical, 45; funerals, 88; majority, 25; teens, 65
puberty, 81–83

Quakers, 25, 92–93, 95, 100

Reboot, 13, 66
reincarnation, 93–94, 99, 103
religious liberty, 17
Religious Society of Friends. *See* Quakers
religious symbols, 20, 24, 126
right-to-die, 38, 48
Roe v. Wade, 46
rumspringa, 85

sabbath, 62–63, 73, 102
Santeria, 105
school prayer, 26
Scientologists, 95, 104
Seventh-Day Adventists, 8, 73
Sikh, 61–62, 125
Soul Searching: The Religious and Spiritual Lives of American Teenagers, 65
Southern Poverty Law Center (SPLC), 41–42
Spiritualist, 24
spirituality, 3–5, 75, 77–78, 105, 125–26
stem cells, 38, 46–48, 50

Teen Spirit: One World, Many Paths, 125
Ten Commandments, 21–24
theocracy, 20, 39
turbans, 1, 61–62

Unitarian Universalists, 5, 13, 95, 104, 113, 116, 122, 125
U.S. Supreme Court, 19, 23–26, 31, 37, 46, 54, 56–58, 60, 86–87, 116

vouchers, school, 26, 31–33

"wall of separation," 18–19
Wiccans, 5, 28, 53, 88, 95–98, 123, 125

Zelman v. Simmons-Harris, 32–33
Zoroastrians, 95, 104, 125

About the Author

Kathlyn Gay is the author of more than one hundred books that focus on social and environmental issues, culture, history, communication, and sports for a variety of audiences. Some of her books have been written in collaboration with family members. A full-time freelance author, Kathlyn has also published hundreds of magazine features and stories, plays, and promotional materials, and she has written and contributed to encyclopedias, teachers' manuals, and textbooks. She and her husband, Arthur, are Florida residents.